Battleground Europe

THE
HINDENBURG LINE

Battleground Europe

THE
HINDENBURG LINE

Peter Oldham

Series editor
Nigel Cave

LEO COOPER
London

First published in 1997 by
LEO COOPER
190 Shaftesbury Avenue, London WC2H 8JL
an imprint of
Pen Sword Books Limited
47 Church Street, Barnsley, South Yorkshire S70 2AS

ISBN 0 85052 568 3

A CIP catalogue of this book is available
from the British Library

Printed by Redwood Books Limited
Trowbridge, Wiltshire

*For up-to-date information on other titles produced under the Leo
Cooper imprint, please telephone or write to:*

Pen & Sword Books Ltd, FREEPOST, 47 Church Street
Barnsley, South Yorkshire S70 2AS
Telephone 01226 734222

CONTENTS

ACKNOWLEDGEMENTS

I am greatly indebted to a large number of people who have provided help, information, advice, tea and sympathy in the preparation of this book. To the Imperial War Museum and many regimental museums and county record offices I owe a debt of gratitude for the chance to delve into their archives, especially Maggie Magnuson and the ladies of the Royal Engineers Library, Chatham, and various public libraries, particularly those of Saffron Walden and Cambridge. Brian Morgan of Great Chesterford has been very helpful in the production of maps, and Aleks Deseyne of Wondelgem has provided some contemporary photographs. Trevor Pidgeon and Paul Hanson of the Western Front Association have, as ever, been very helpful with the supply of trench maps for field visits. Many thanks to Comte de Francqueville at La Folie and to Baron de Valicourt at Flesquières for access and hospitality, and many other kind farmers and landowners. A special debt is owed to Pierre Capelle of Trescault for his unrivalled local knowledge, freely shared, and for time given in traipsing through woods and fields and sharing bottles of beer at lunchtime; also to Mireille for some excellent French food and hospitality. Nothing would be possible without Jennifer, who has provided encouragement and patience.

The Hindenburg Line: thick belts of wire defending a tunnel at Bellicourt. Gaps in the wire have been created by the British barrage, 1918.

SERIES INTRODUCTION

This book is the first of the **Battleground Europe** series to look at what the British called the Hindenburg Line. Most visitors to the battlefields today concentrate first and foremost on the Somme and then on the Ypres Salient. The area south of Armentières, where the great British offensive battles on the Western Front of 1915 were largely fought, and the area to the south of Arras to the Somme have suffered similar neglect.

The third area which sees few visitors to is the east of Arras and around Cambrai and St Quentin. Peter Oldham's book puts this right, by providing a vade mecum to the great series of defences to which the Germans withdrew in the early months of 1917. The Battle of Arras has been overshadowed by Third Ypres for reasons that are far from apparent. Cambrai is heard of but rarely studied; whilst the various offensives of 1918, German and allied, seem to be studied but not visited on the ground. Perhaps this is because it is an area that has not been well covered in the literature (though books such as the masterly *Kaiser's Battle*, by Martin Middlebrook and Jonathon Nicholl's *Cheerful Sacrifice* should have rectified that). Certainly it cannot be for lack of remnants of that period – there are great numbers of concrete fortifications still remaining. Perhaps it is because there has not been a detailed enough book on the subject.

If that is the case then this book must go a long way to satisfying this need. Peter Oldham looks at the area, dividing it into manageable sections and explains its importance. He does this with the aid of clear maps, which enables visitors to orientate themselves and to follow the events that took place there over eighty and more years ago. Remaining bunkers are frequently put into the context of the battle so that it is possible to follow some of the actions which took place around them, to understand their importance and in many cases to be looking at a structure whose capture or defence earned a heroic man – or men – the Victoria Cross.

Besides all of this Mr Oldham explains the genesis, development and occupation of the Line, as well as the battles which took place there. For many years it has been unfashionable to consider that Britain and her Dominions could possibly be winning a war on military merit. This book goes a long way to proving that this was the case; and at the same time makes it clear that this was a most notable achievement.

It is quite certain that this book will bring many visitors to see this part of the Great War Battlefield. It might be a little late, but at long last the men who fought and died here have now got a worthy guide to their exploits. Those who lie in the cemeteries around Cambrai and St Quentin or whose names are commemorated on the various memorials are quite likely to have more visitors thanks to this book; visitors who will be rather more aware of what and when it was that they suffered the supreme price.

It is to be expected that this is just the first of a number of books in the **Battleground Europe** series about the battles and events on and around the Hindenburg Line. Doubtless this book will whet the appetite of the reader for such works.

Nigel Cave
Ely Place, London

INTRODUCTION

On the morning of 6 February 1917, pilot Lieutenant Peters and his observer, Lieutenant Balfour, of 70 Squadron R.F.C. were flying their Sopwith at a height of 4,000 metres (13,000 feet) on a reconnaissance mission over St. Quentin. Visibility was good, and below them they noticed that the town was being organised for defence. On landing they presented a report on their findings:

'There appears to be a complete system of trenches around the town. On the south east corner of the town there is a short line about 3/4-1 mile running up through Itancourt. On the north side, running east of the canal, is a fairly continuous line with strongpoints at about 1/4 mile intervals. Between Bellicourt and Bellenglise the line of trenches is very broken.'

This report confirmed earlier gleanings of information from intelligence sources but was the first real proof of enemy activity in this area since the previous autumn, when defence work to the north, around Quèant, had been noticed but not much importance had been attached to this. Other reconnaissance flights followed and the British began to build a picture of what lay before them: the strongest system of scientifically designed defences that the world had then seen. The search for further knowledge and details increased as the British planners tried to understand the nature of the defences and the way in which they might be used. Trench raids were carried out by the infantry to gain information, prisoners were interrogated and escaped civilians, some repatriated through Switzerland, were quizzed. The R.F.C. were given the task of identifying the whole system and flew countless sorties, taking many thousands of photographs whilst also carrying out bombing raids on the transport lines.

Even when they had a good idea of the amount of work put in by the Germans, the British had no reason to suspect that their intention was to evacuate the ground which they had so stubbornly defended during the Battle of the Somme. Unaware of the political and military thoughts behind the decision the British were taken by surprise by the German initiative.

The 1917 Battles of Arras, Bullecourt and Cambrai were to show that there was a limit to the ground the Germans were willing to cede and any ground won would have to be fiercely fought for. Falling back onto the position in the autumn of 1918, with their plans and hopes dashed and fatigued after four years of warfare, the Germans were to make one last stand to prevent the British and French reaching the Fatherland.

During the course of the several battles in and around the Hindenburg Line both sides developed and improved tactics of attack and defence: necessity was the mother of invention and tank warfare, unregistered artillery bombardments, shell proof protection, elastic defence and the use of storm troops to infiltrate defences were all perfected.

The Hindenburg Line was also to become as strong in the minds of the British public as it was on the ground, being given almost mythical status in the newspapers. Church bells rang when the line was pierced at Cambrai in 1917 and the crossing of the St. Quentin Canal by the 46th Division in September 1918 was seen as a master stroke which presaged the end of the war.

Visitors to the area today are likely to find, at first sight, little or nothing to tell them that the land was once a maze of trenches too wide for a tank to cross, with hundreds of mined dug-outs and acres and acres of barbed wire. Even the permanent constructions: thick reinforced concrete shelters and pill boxes for machine-guns, command posts and artillery crews can be difficult to find, often being

Because they were built at trench level many of the remaining vestiges are difficult to find and identify, especially when crops are growing. The occupants of this bunker, (rough ground in centre) near Bellicourt, held up the British advance in 1917, directed fire onto the British at the start of the 1918 spring offensive, it then poured fire into the Americans and Australians in September 1918. As with many similar sites it is much easier to find in winter.

Bunkers, observation posts, etc. are in many villages, but not always immediately apparent. This bunker built into a garden wall in Banteux was a German command post, and was used by the British who planned how to cross the canal 200 metres away.

identifiable only as a patch of coarse grass and weeds in a ploughed field, for the defences were generally built at trench level with the roof hidden by a thin layer of soil. Some vestiges are obvious, tall observation posts for artillery observers of both sides are can be found in villages and fields, and the other permanent reminders of the protracted fighting – the many cemeteries, sometimes isolated and rarely visited – tell their own story. Divisional memorials, erected in honour of fallen comrades by veterans, can also be found at some important sites.

The area may not have the tourist appeal of the Somme and Ypres, but for the interested visitor much can be seen to gain an impression of its former condition and gain an idea of the events which took place here. It is also simple to visit the sites of action and anguish on both sides and to perceive the occurrence of great deeds.

Whilst most of the land is arable and large expanses of beet, cereals and other crops cover the fields, ploughing still brings up an assortment of debris, but it is in the woods, generally untouched by plough or harrow, that a best impression can be gained. Much of the ground will be found to be broken still, with shell holes, trenches (fallen in and

fairly shallow but often easily identifiable and traceable) and collapsed dug-outs. Sometimes barbed wire – usually the thicker German variety – will be found hanging from trees, nailed there to prevent passage and hinder attackers. As on other sectors of the Western Front, unexploded shells and grenades are frequently seen. They should not be touched but left well alone.

The area in the triangle Arras-Cambrai-St. Quentin is attractive rolling chalk downland; villages are often unremarkable, having few if any aged buildings. Many of the villages contain shelters, bunkers and other constructions which have survived later developments but these can be very difficult or impossible to find or visit.

The woods in the area often have traces of defences and show signs of the fighting. From the tree in the photo above hangs five rows of German barbed wire, now higher than when nailed to the tree.

The time of year makes a definite difference to the nature of the landscape and the ability to picture events. In the long days of summer, with extended evenings, travel is easy and walking the fields is enjoyable (a good way to work off all that good French food and wine) but shrubbery and herbage masks many features. In the winter, and especially the spring, daylight hours are reduced but the land is easier to identify; hills and valleys, so important to attackers and defenders, become apparent and ground level bunkers and dug-outs become more easily identifiable.

This book is not intended to be a critical analysis of battles fought in the area, or a treatise on the strategies of generals. There is available a wealth of books on both these topics by competent authors. Nor is it meant to be an in-depth story of the events at any one location; again there are books, such as *A Wood Called Bourlon* by Moore[1] and *Cambrai* by Smithers[2], which go into greater detail for specific events. Whilst giving an overview of both German and British strategy and

Many of the woods show much evidence of the defences and the fighting, with shell holes, collapsed dug-outs and trenches. The British trench above – Ivry Trench – is in Fig Wood, near Holnon, it was part of the forward defences manned by the 2/8th Worcesters and 61 Battalion, Machine Gun Corps when the Germans attacked on 21 March 1918. Hand-to-hand fighting took place here before the Germans forced the British back.

tactics the book does not attempt to cover these in detail.

It is intended as a general guide to the region in which the British troops had some major trials and tribulations, an area into which, apart from one or two sites, few battlefield visitors venture. The maps are designed to give the visitor, or armchair reader, an impression of what events took place in each small area, together with an appreciation of the manner in which defence lines changed hands. The maps contain the main trench lines but it must be borne in mind that these sometimes grew and diminished in importance as lines changed, whilst trench names also changed from time to time. Communication and support lines were more liable to change, and, being much more numerous, are difficult to show on maps without obscuring detail. Omitted from the maps are some cemeteries, most of these are shown on Michelin and I.G.N. (Institute Geographique National) maps and visitors are recommended to use one of these in addition.

Reference numbers for the I.G.N. 1:25000 (Blue Series) I.G.N. maps, which give good topographical detail as well as showing military cemeteries, are: 2406 E, 2506 O, 2506 E, 2606 O, 2507 O, 2507 E, 2607 O, 2508 E, 2608 O,2509 E, and 2609 O. The Western Front Association has an excellent trench map service for members.

The map for each section does show what is believed to be every remaining construction of the defence lines which became known as the Hindenburg Line (except for some which have been deliberately left out in accordance with landowners requests, and some in Cambrai town) together with the British remains in the region. Doubtless one or two have been missed but these will not be many. More important are those which have been found and photographed, only to disappear as a roadway, housing or industrial development occurs. More are buried or destroyed each year by the farmers on whose land they sit. It is regretted if one is marked on the map but is found not to be there now.

The maps also show some centres of interest, where specific deeds, such as the winning of a VC or major action, took place. The list of such deeds is, of course, almost endless, as over a million men fought and died here in several major battles and not all can be included. The boundaries of the maps are purely arbitrary, battles did not conveniently follow maps and later battles make it more complicated, but for each map the principal events which took place are given.

It is hoped that the armchair reader will be able to follow the events in comfort; it is also hoped that the battlefield visitor, with the aid of this book, will be able to visit any site – a village perhaps, a wood or the remains of a concrete monolith in the middle of a field – and will have an appreciation of the events which occured here in 1917 and 1918.

The Hindenburg Line: wire in front of the Beaurevoir Line, 1918.

ADVICE TO TRAVELLERS

The area in the triangle Arras/Cambrai/St Quentin is pleasant gentle rolling chalk downland, with largely arable farmland separating the villages. The countryside is often large vistas of crops or empty ploughed land; many of the hedgerows and copses have been cleared for agricultural purposes. Access to most sites is not difficult as the land has a network of tracks and small roads, however the visitor should be prepared to do some walking to gain the best impressions of defences and movements. Hence stout shoes, or wellingtons in wet weather (the Somme and Ypres were not the only places where mud was a problem!) are useful, as is suitable clothing for the weather. Some advice on the best time of year to visit is given in the Introduction, but all seasons have their merits.

The majority of the villages are unremarkable, being working agricultural rather than dormitory or weekend communities, and few old or interesting buildings will be seen as most were demolished during the war. The visitor is not catered for and accommodation and lunch is hard to find, to make the most of the day a picnic lunch is advised.

Hotels of all categories can be found in Arras, Cambrai and St Quentin; as can a wide range of restaurants. Some hotels found to be particularly convenient and inexpensive are the hotels of the Formule 1 chain to be found on the outskirts of Arras and Cambrai. The one on the outskirts of Arras, on the road to Cambrai, is where the battlefields have been swallowed by the growth of the town. The one outside Cambrai, at the A2 Motorway access at Fontaine-Notre-Dame, is on the Bapaume road (the hotel is on the site of the Marcoing Line). Adjacent is the Hotel Ibis. For campers and caravanners, a good site is at Boiry-Notre-Dame, close to Monchy-le-Preux.

Whilst the visitor should have a pleasant and informative time in visiting the sites of the actions and battles covered in this book, it should be remembered that most of the land is owned by somebody and whereas access is unlikely to be denied, normal courtesy, in the form of not leaving litter and closing gates, should be shown. In addition to the obvious danger from the numerous unexploded shells and grenades, which should be left well alone, some woods and open land are the domain of French game and bird shooters and care should be exercised.

CHAPTER ONE

The situation in the winter of 1916/17 and German plans for withdrawal to a new defence line.

The Battle of the Somme ground to a halt in the middle of November, 1916; the winter weather set in with a vengeance and both sides, weakened and with horrendous manpower losses, set up front line defences which were thinly held. The French Armies were exhausted and depleted after their fights at Verdun and needed time to re-equip and re-man. The Germans, who apart from material and troop losses, had major problems of morale at both troop and staff levels after their hitherto military superiority had taken a beating. The British, counting the dead after four months of battle, discussed whether the Somme campaign had been a success or failure. This debate is yet unfinished – the German army had been worn down and was shaken by the experience, and the battle was 'one of the foundation stones on which the advance to victory in 1918 was built'[3]. However the original carefree fighting spirit of the British soldier had been broken: he had lost his idealism and was from now on not an enthusiastic volunteer.

For eight weeks after the end of the battle the conditions in the trenches were appalling – continuous rain, sleet and snow meant that mud – which had been a deciding factor in breaking off the active offensive operations – caused almost all movement to become impossible. Moving parts of guns and rifles ceased to function, trench collapses meant that communication trenches were impassable and men were frequently buried by mud slides. Most troops were withdrawn to rear areas for rest and re-fitting, whilst troops holding the front line suffered much sickness and trench foot became a major type of complaint. Although the front lines were only thinly held some activity did not cease – patrols went out on most nights into No Man's Land, often capturing prisoners, sniping remained an ever present danger and artillery shelling continued.

The British maintained their policy of being aggressive and did not allow any Christmas goodwill to interfere: at mid-day on 25 December all guns on the Somme front fired a salvo at likely German gathering points. This 'Christian' act – intended both to maintain pressure on the Germans and to inhibit any fraternisation – was repugnant to many British soldiers. It was repeated on the stroke of the New Year on December 31.

Infantry trench raids and patrols continued in earnest over the first few days of January 1917; many prisoners were taken by British battalions, although many of these turned out to be willing deserters. Some German attacks were carried out, such as where the 7th Division's Hope Post, near Beaumont Hamel, was taken from the 9th Devons, the loss being discovered by two Devons officers approaching the post with rum rations for the garrison. The initiative generally lay with the British who maintained the offensive. For the first full attack of 1917, against Muck Trench and the Triangle, a trench system near Serre, the attackers had to carry duck boards to enable them to cross the mud. In the middle of January 1917 the weather changed; sub-zero temperatures and heavy frosts set in and the ground froze hard and solid. Sickness rates became even higher than before, special arrangements were made for the supply of clean, warm and dry clothing and R.A.M.C. centres were kept busy.

The freezing of the ground changed some operational methods, with more movement after dark over the open ground as water-filled shell holes and deep mud ceased to be traps. Trench walls, now the ground was solid, did not collapse, and heavy falls of snow necessitated the issue of white overalls for night patrols. The snow on the ground also enabled artillery observers on both sides to determine which trenches, tracks, dugouts and posts were used and manned, and to direct their fire accordingly: 'harassing fire on both sides became noticeably more precise'.[4]

Over the course of the winter months the planners on both sides of the front had been busy. Generals Haig and Robertson had met with the the French Commander-in-Chief, General Joffre at Chantilly in mid November 1916; they agreed to resume hostilities with the Germans as soon as the weather improved, hopefully in February. The British were to attack on a front from the north of the Somme battlefield, the French were to tackle the Germans south of Peronne.

While plans were being made some changes were made at the top which meant that such arrangements would need to be halted and re-started. Lloyd George replaced Asquith as British Prime Minister, which had a big effect upon General Haig's ability to direct the British effort, and General Joffre was promoted out of battle planning in favour of General Nivelle who had what was thought to be the answer to the deadlock on French soil. This answer involved new methods of attack and the subordination of the British Army to the French.

The Germans also had some major changes of personnel which resulted in changes in strategy and tactics from those which had been used during the earlier parts of the 1916 summer fighting. General von

Falkenhayn, who had directed the German effort, was sent off to Rumania, and Field Marshal Hindenburg, with Ludendorff at his side, was put in charge of the O.H.L. (German High Command). Hindenburg and Ludendorff immediately changed German tactics: the fighting at Verdun was scaled down to allow a much greater concentration of resources in the one area and front line trenches were now not to be held necessarily at all costs but could be given up when considered appropriate. The German First Army chief of staff, Colonel von Lossberg, was also able to form a body of reserve divisions in the back areas to be brought forward to relieve front divisions when necessary. Lossberg was also able to organise defences of a less rigid type than hitherto, fighting would now take place in a deep zone which gave the best advantage to the defenders, rather than a front line trench which could be destroyed by enemy artillery. Thus the Battle of the Somme ground to a halt with the early trial use of defence in depth.

The experiences and information gained during these later actions were considered by Lossberg. His conclusions were then used by General von Below to produce a record of the changes during the battle: *Erfahrungen der 1 Armee in der Sommeschlacht* (Experiences of the First Army in the Somme Battle). This document, printed on 30 January 1917, explained the concept of a mobile defence in depth and was to become very important in future German defence strategies for the rest of the war.

During the winter of 1916/17 the overall situation on the Western Front convinced Hindenburg and Ludendorff that a period of stable defence was required in order to allow conditions to improve. The eastern front was still active – Russia was still not yet defeated and Rumania had now joined the Allies, which meant that almost half (122 out of a total of 255 divisions) of the German forces were in the east. German industry was by now running flat out on the war effort but there was a shortage of many essential materials, the potato harvest had failed and the German people were beginning to suffer hunger.

The decision was therefore made to try and bring the war to an end by starving Britain of food and essential supplies, bringing Britain to its knees and cutting the channel link with France. This would be brought about by unrestricted submarine warfare which was was ordered on 9 January and announced on 31 January: the U-boat campaign was to begin in full force on 1 February and from then on no vessel – naval or civilian, Allied or neutral, would be safe.

Meanwhile German defence tactics had been re-assessed, and plans which had been hatched earlier were now put into operation. This included the perfection of an idealised defensive zone, with artillery observation from the rear, and carefully sited trench lines on reverse slopes to prevent British artillery observation. The order for the construction of such a position had been given soon after Hindenburg and Ludendorff took command, on 5 September 1916. The area behind the German army on the Somme was to be the first of five such major defences and was the first to be sited and traced out as it would give the most benefit in terms of release of man power, as the battle had created a large bulge in the German lines.

The defence zone or *stellung* was given the name *Siegfried* after one of the heroes of the Teutonic sagas. *Siegfried* was originally a descendant of the god Odin in the Scandinavian *Volsunga* Saga but was adopted into German folklore in the *Nibelungenlied*, a medieval poem written about 1200.

The construction and maintenance of roads and railway lines to feed the front with troops, guns and ammunition required much manpower. When the Hindenburg Line was planned the reduction in the length of front was expected to reduce the demand for men and munitions. These troops are repairing a line at Rethel, well behind the front, for the supply of construction materials for the new defence lines.

The godly associations were timely, the Siegfried cycle by Wagner was in its fortieth year, having been first produced at Bayreuth in 1876. The *Siegfriedstellung* was sited to run from Arras to St. Quentin and then continue down past Laon to the Aisne, cutting off a large salient which was to be abandoned. Other sectors of the Western Front were to follow and most of these new defence systems were also to be named after German gods. The Wotan Line (*Wotan-stellung*) ran northwards from the Siegfried line at Quèant up to Drocourt and Lille from where it continued to the coast at Ostend as the *Flandernstellung* or Flanders Line.

The *Hundingstellung* or Hunding Line ran from the *Siegfriedstellung* at la Fère and then behind the Champagne battlefields; east of that *Michelstellung* was to cut out the Saint Mihiel salient.

When the British followed the Germans as they retired to the new line all accommodation and billeting had been destroyed and rapid building was required. This was also the case when the British pushed the Germans back from their defences in 1917. The troops above are constructing shelters on the edge of Havrincourt Wood in the winter of 1917/18. The road is the D15 from Trescault.

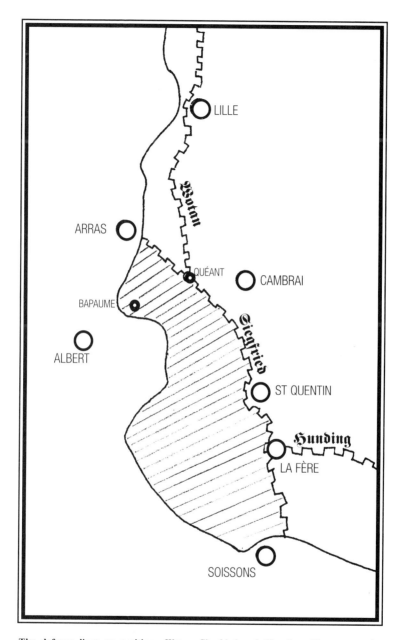

LILLE

Wotan

ARRAS

QUÉANT

CAMBRAI

BAPAUME

Siegfried

ALBERT

ST QUENTIN

Hunding

LA FÈRE

SOISSONS

The defence lines or positions *Wotan*, *Siegfried* and *Hunding*. The area to be evacuated, shown shaded, was systematically destroyed during the withdrawal to ensure that nothing remained which might be of use to British troops.

The *Siegfriedstellung* – which would later be named the Hindenburg Line by the British – was a hundred and forty four kilometers (ninety miles) long and would cut out forty kilometers (twenty five miles) of German front. The idea of shortening the front had been instigated by General-leutnant Fuchs at Cambrai. By 19 September its general course had been agreed and traced out. On 27 September the order for construction work to begin was given by Crown Prince Rupprecht of Bavaria, commanding the Army Group. The siting of the *Wotanstellung*, which was to join at Quéant, was agreed on 4 November but work was not to start until the *Siegfriedstellung* was almost complete, to enable the best use of resources.

The construction of the defensive zone had been agreed as a precautionary measure only. As late as January 1917 it was considered that the front line would be held unless a British attack forced it back. By the end of January it had become clear to Crown Prince Rupprecht that his front and rear lines could not withstand a British spring offensive, and he considered that one was likely when weather permitted. He recommended on 28 January to Ludendorff that the line be withdrawn and the *Siegfriedstellung* be occupied. The plan was rejected for both political and strategic reasons, although later consideration of the benefits of such a withdrawal – mainly the fact that it would free thirteen infantry divisions and many artillery batteries – made Ludendorff rethink the situation. Another major factor which caused Ludendorff to change his mind was news of serious delays in the delivery of munitions. He had been advised that supplies would be well below expectation and time was still needed to replenish supplies of guns and artillery ammunition.

On 4 February 1917 the order to prepare for withdrawal to the Hindenburg Line was given, and for construction work on the system to continue as rapidly as possible. The operation, named *Alberich* after the malignant dwarf who curses the holders of the ring in Wagner's opera, was to begin on 9 February 1917. The actual withdrawal, over the three days 15-18 March, was to be preceded by five weeks of total devastation of the area to be evacuated, although many senior army commanders, including Crown Prince Rupprecht, opposed this part of the plan on moral grounds.

The intention was to deny the British any use of buildings or land in the wake of the withdrawal. All military and civilian shelter was to be demolished, railways torn up, trees cut down (roadside trees were felled across the road as barriers and fruit trees to remove any source of food). Wells, upon which the British were expected to be dependant for water, were blown in. Later British reports talk of wells polluted with horse dung and creosote and even of poisoning. Although many Royal Engineer units reported on the work to clear wells, no confirmed cases of poisoning were found. This has not prevented later accounts of the war claiming this as commonplace. It is likely that the poisoning of water, if it did occur (in direct contra-vention of the Hague Convention and therefore punishable) was an isolated event which gave rise to unsubstantiated and very exaggerated rumours.

The orgy of destruction was disliked by some Germans although many appear to have lusted in it, committing some deeds (such as the desecration of graves in Cartigny Cemetery) of no military value. Ernst Jünger, in *Storm of Steel* justifies such actions from the point of view of a Prussian officer:

'The country over which the enemy were to advance had been turned into an utter desolation. The moral justification of this has been much discussed. However, it seems to me that the gratified approval of arm-chair warriors and journalists is incomprehensible. When thousands of peaceful persons are robbed of their homes, the self-satisfaction of power may at least keep silence. As for the necessity, I have of course, as a Prussian officer, no doubt whatever. War is the harshest of all trades, and masters of it can only entertain humane feelings so long as they do no harm.'[5]

The laying of booby traps and delayed action explosives was commonplace and were carefully and skillfully done so as to kill as many troops as possible whilst slowing down the pursuit. Booby traps included trip wires in trenches, dugouts and cellars and were connected to souvenirs, doorways and obstacles likely to be moved. These were arranged to explode charges or grenades. The body of a British soldier

Few places were found to be free of traps. This example was one of many found in trenches: a soldier stepping on the loose trench board would set off the charge connected to it.

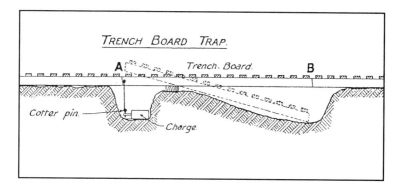

was found with a percussion device attached by wire to the wrist and many explosives were found in chimneys and stoves, liable to be set off when a fire was lit.

Road junctions and railway lines had been blown up but many were left with delay action fuses for later damage and disruption. These fuses were fired by a number of methods: clockwork, the eating away of a wire by acid and percussion or friction such as mines laid in a road cavity with a thin layer of earth over, to be set off by passing traffic.

The Germans expended much effort to make the many traps and mines effective and they certainly did hinder the British. Some Royal Engineer Companies spent most of the next few months searching buildings, cellars, dugouts, roads, bridges, rubble and fields for explosives instead of improving transport and communications and organising defences. Delays at road junctions, bridges and railways meant that infantry had to travel overland without artillery and supplies of ammunition, food and water. Not all searches were successful and there were casualties. One such occurrence was at Bapaume Town Hall: the cellars were searched and a mine found and removed as soon as the Australians entered the town. Eight days later a large explosion, caused by a mine with a delayed fuse, a steel wire suspended in acid was slowly corroded, after which it released a spring activating a detonator, brought down the tower and masonry onto about thirty Australian troops and workers of the Australian Comforts Fund, together with two visiting French officials, Captain R. Briquet and M. Albert Taillander. Soon after another similar system blew up the nearby headquarters of 7 Australian Brigade.

The numerous types of traps resulted in the issuing to engineers and infantry of a booklet, *Hints on Reconnaissance for Mines and Land Mines in the Area Evacuated by the Germans*[6]. The information and experience gained was to come in handy again. When the Germans were falling back over the same area in August and September 1918 the same tactics of delay and damage were used, resulting in another advisory document *German Traps and Mines*. Royal Engineer Companies were again required to clear all dugouts, billets and shelter before use by troops, some finding several hundreds of booby traps and mines including some in seemingly innocent locations. The 11th Division reported finding two graves marked 'to an unknown soldier' ; on investigation they proved to contain explosives with delayed action fuses[7].

As in 1917, traps and mines were not always placed in obvious places, and the unwary were in danger. Engineer Companies, such as 182 Tunnelling Company, recorded their findings, for example:

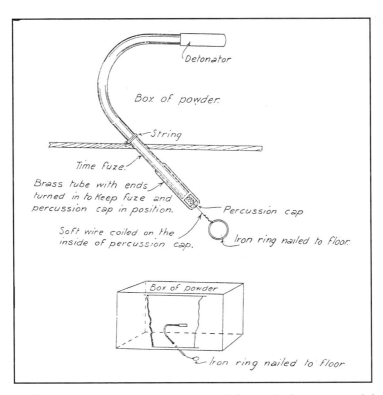

The Royal Engineers, dealing with thousands of German booby traps, recorded some examples. The Box Trap above was a box of Perdite (explosive powder) set to be detonated when the box was lifted.

'One of our Stokes mortar shells had been converted into a booby trap, and placed in a heap of bricks along the road. A tape and spring which was fixed so as to release the striking pin and fire the shell was attached to a piece of timber on top of the bricks'[8].

The setters of the trap knew that a soldier would be foraging for wood at some stage.

Whilst many British troops were indignant, finding the use of such devices repugnant, the British themselves had left similar devices for the Turks on evacuating Gallipoli and also during later local withdrawals: orders for the evacuation of Bourlon Wood in early December, 1917 included the demolition of anything which might be of use to the Germans and 'if booby traps and other devices for inflicting loss on the enemy can be improvised it would be an advantage'.[9] The British retreat of March 1918 included the demolition of roads, railways and bridges, and the syllabus for the R.E. School of Instruction at Rouen included lectures on 'Organisation of Arrangements for Demolition in case of Retirement'.[10]

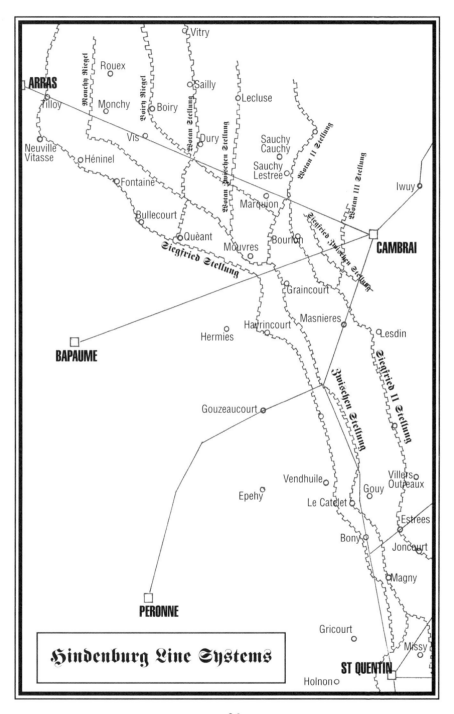

Vitry

Rouex

ARRAS

Tilloy

Monchy

Sailly

Boiry

Lecluse

Vis

Dury

Sauchy
Cauchy

Iwuy

Neuville
Vitasse

Héninel

Sauchy
Lestree

Fontaine

Marquion

Bullecourt

CAMBRAI

Quèant

Mouvres

Bourlon

Siegfried Stellung

Graincourt

Masnieres

Harrincourt

Lesdin

BAPAUME

Hermies

Gouzeaucourt

Villers
Outreaux

Vendhuile

Gouy

Epehy

Le Catelet

Estrees

Bony

Joncourt

Magny

PERONNE

Gricourt

Missy

Hindenburg Line Systems

ST QUENTIN

Holnon

The successive systems of the Hindenburg Line. Each of the *Stellung* systems shown is a series of between two and five fire trenches with communication trenches, artillery observation posts and batteries, machine-gun emplacements, shell proof infantry accomodation, command and aid posts. Each system was fronted by thick belts of barbed wire, in bands of up to 20 metres depth; in front of this were listening and picket posts. The *Riegel* lines were simpler systems, comprising two or three trenches (*Graben*) for infantry with machine-guns and trench mortars. These were also heavily protected by barbed wire. Communication and connecting trenches were usually named as *weg* (or way), e.g. *Kaiserweg* and *Königsweg*. Individual strongpoints and posts were called *werk*, e.g. *Hanseatenwerk*.

The more numerous systems in the northern part of the area were due to changes and developments during the Battles of Arras and Cambrai in 1917. The southern sector was not tested until the later battles in September and October, 1918, when the Germans were falling back and not in a position to re-align or change the layout.

The Germans had named their defence systems after mythical characters, but the British names for them were rather more prosaic. Whereas Hindenburg, the German *Commandant*, was honoured by the British, who adopted his name, most trenches were named after their geographical location, usually the nearest villages, i.e.:

Wotanstellung – Drocourt-Quèant Line

Wotan II Stellung – Canal du Nord Line

Zwischenstellung or Intermediate line – Le Catelet and Graincourt Lines.

Siegfried II Stellung – Masnières-Beaurevoir-Fonsommes Line

Siegfried II Zwischenstellung – Marcoing Line

Other German lines – *Hunding, Hermann, Fafner, Brunhild* – were given similarly uninspired names by the British

CHAPTER TWO

Construction of the *Siegfriedstellung*

Even as the Germans were retiring to the *Siegfriedstellung* they were changing their minds about the best methods of defence and the way in which the position was to be used. The design was for two roughly parallel trenches, 200 metres apart, the front trench or *sicherheitsbesatzung* for the sentries and forward troops and the second trench or *hauptverteidigungslinie* for the main body of infantry. Machine guns, in shell proof shelters, mainly reinforced concrete, were located in front of and behind the second trench, sited to sweep the approaches and ground in front with their field of fire. Broad belts of barbed wire, up to fifty metres wide, were laid in front of the first trench, not parallel to the trench as in earlier defence lines but laid in patterns which would channel attacking troops into the best zones for the machine gun crews to fire at them. Between 500 and 1000 metres behind the trenches, which were sited mainly on the reverse slopes of hills (*hinterhangstellung*), and machine gun positions, allowing minimum fields of view to the attackers, were the artillery observation posts, which directed artillery fire from batteries further back, upon the attackers approaching the barbed wire. Many of these observation posts also had fields of view which provided artillery information for areas behind the British lines and so could bring shell fire down on British transport and troop movements. The siting of the system also denied observation over the German lines to the British.

The labour and material requirements for the carrying out of the works imposed a load on the Germans abilities to man existing defences and construct all of the planned projects. Manpower was drafted in from all available sources: Russian prisoners of war, French and Belgian civilian forced labour, engineering and pioneer companies and many infantry working parties were involved. Most of the more complicated work, such as laying and improving railways and tunnelling for dug-outs, was carried out by reserve troops, *Reservepionier-kompanie* and *Landsturminfanteriebataillone*; in some areas *Marinekorps*, who had been engaged in constructing coastal batteries on the Belgian coast, were used. Civilian contractors with skilled German workers were employed on much of the concrete work for machine gun emplacements and bunkers. Each sector had standard patterns of gun emplacement, observation post and bunker so that workshops could mass produce and pre-fabricate many of the components. Some of the constructing units, obviously proud of their handiwork, left plaques and name plates on their constructions. Two examples – one for *III bayer Pioneer Kompanie* and one for *Marine Kompanie 19* – can be found near Banteaux.

A German civilian contractor outside a recently completed concrete bunker. The trees in the background are on the Bonavis-La Vaquerie track, later cleared during agricultural development. Inset is the bunker today, one of several of the same pattern which can be found around Lateau Wood near the Cambrai-St. Quentin road.

Large quantities of construction materials – cement, steel, sand and gravel – were brought up to build the bunkers and pill boxes. This rail depot at Fontaine-les-Croisilles, operated by *bayer Landsturminfanteriebataill. 2 Munchen*, who constructed the defences between this village and Héninel, included a workshop where steel reinforcing bars were bent to shape, wooden formwork was cut to size, and goods re-loaded onto light railways and horse drawn transport. The site is occupied today by the village football pitch (inset).

When the line was sited and taped out the layout was as agreed by the *Oberste Heeresleitung* O.H.L., (or Supreme Command), i.e. two trenches about 200 metres apart. Construction of the defences was well advanced when a change of idea was adopted. The Chief of Staff of the German First Army, Colonel Fritz von Lossberg (described in the British Official History as 'a very remarkable soldier'[11] decided he did not like or agree with the layout and the intended use of the defence scheme. He had found that the front trench system was often on a forward rather than reverse slope and artillery observation was very limited; moreover artillery observation posts were often in the front line and sometimes in front of the line, making them vulnerable to British artillery and liable to have reduced vision from dust and smoke in battle. Lossberg insisted on having artillery observation posts well behind the immediate battlefield. He determined that by re-positioning the front line trenches to about 2,500 metres in front of the proposed

Long lengths of trench were excavated, with many tunnelled |dug-outs for shelter and accommodation. The dug-outs being mined above, on Héninel Hill, were all connected, allowing the German infantry and machine gunners to appear where needed. When these were captured by the 18th Manchesters other British troops, wounded prisoners, were found inside.

front trench with an outpost line (*Vorpostenfeld*) in front of this, the position was made much stronger. Accordingly a shift forward (*Vorverlegung*) began over much of the line. The original Hindenburg Line became the Hindenburg Support Line (*Siegfried Zwischenstellung*) and artillery protection line (the *Artillerie-schutzstellung*). Artillery batteries, machine guns and infantry were re-deployed until a broad belt of defences were in place, the system then consisted of a forward or outpost zone between the outpost and first main trench, and a battle zone between the new front line and the original Hindenburg Line. The defence scheme now meant that the attacking British, once past the outpost line, would be out of the sight of their own artillery observation and would therefore not have artillery support, but were in full sight of German artillery, machine gunners and infantry. Some of the machine guns were close behind the front trench whilst others were scattered around the battle zone in strategic strongpoints (*Widastands-nester*).

The defence system had therefore shifted from a line of trenches to be defended one by one to a zonal system which an attacker might penetrate but would be unable to pass through for any distance. To allow for the limited penetration a number of battalions and regiments of reserve troops (*Sturmbataillone* and *Sturmregimenter*) were kept in the rear to launch a counter-attack (*Gegenangriff*).

As soon as Lossberg and the Supreme Command was satisfied with progress on the organisation of the system the start on another defence line began. This line, also of two trenches with artillery positions, infantry posts and machine guns, was named the *Siegfried II Stellung* (called the Masnières-Beaurevoir and Beaurevoir-Fonsommes Line by the British) and became the rear of the battle zone. More lines, further back, were also contemplated but it was to be only later in 1917 and 1918, when the Germans were really under pressure, that the *Hermann I Stellung* and *Hermann II Stellung* systems were begun.

German engineers concreting a *doppel mebu* (double pill box) for machine gun crews. The design incorporated a pair of thick steel observation posts, one of which can be seen next to the work, ready to be lifted into place and concreted in. The one shown being produced can still be found on Héninel Hill (lower photo).

The British used large calibre guns on railway mountings to destroy important targets well behind the front. The 14″ gun above belonged to a Siege Battery, Royal Garrison Artillery and had a range of thirty kilometres. Three of these were used in the final assault on the Hindenburg Line.

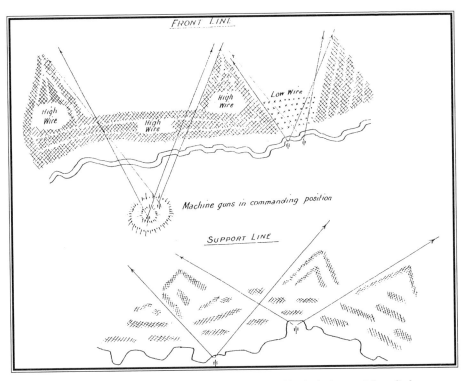

The layout of the Hindenburg defences used belts of barbed wire, on stakes, sited so as to channel attacking infantry into the field of fire of machine guns, usually operating in pairs. In the typical set-up above (from an intelligence report) two guns in the front trench fire over low wire, while two guns further back, on raised ground, fire where attackers would be likely to be. Machine gunners in the support line fired through wire placed to deny passage to any attackers who managed to pass through the front lines. Without the tank the system would have been extremely difficult for the British to penetrate.

The term "Hindenburg Line" is really a misnomer for a defensive system which, when completed, was 6-8,000 metres in depth, with outpost, battle and rear battle zones. The enormous amounts of labour and material expended on it were thought to be well justified in creating an impassible barrier, which could be garrisoned by a minimum of troops, most of them out of the range of British artillery. To be able to reach the German field artillery batteries of 7.7cm to 15cm (the latter known as 5.9″ to the British) guns and howitzers, with a range of between 5,500 and 12,000 metres, the British field artillery of 18 pounders and 4.5 and 6 inch howitzers, with similar ranges, would have to be placed in or beyond the outpost line.

The British realised the great advantage the German artillery had over theirs and sought ways to overcome this. Before the battles of Arras and Cambrai in 1917 an attack had always been preceded by an artillery bombardment, itself preceded by shell firing to register the accuracy of the guns, to cut barbed wire and damage defences; however this also warned the defenders to expect an attack and gave away the locations of the artillery, allowing the defender's artillery to fire upon the attacker's artillery. The combination of the evolution of the tank and unregistered shooting at map co-ordinates (using information from aerial photography, sound ranging and flash spotting, with meteorological adjustments) enabled surprise attacks to consist of the tanks opening up the immediate defences - wire, trenches, infantry and machine guns - for the attacking infantry while the attacking artillery, firing from new positions, knocked out the German artillery. This method, used in an early form at Arras in April, was perfected at Cambrai in November.

Ready for action: German machine gun operator and officer in a strong emplacement.

CHAPTER THREE

British attacks at Arras, Bullecourt and Cambrai in 1917, the German Spring Offensive of March, 1918 and the final British assault on the Hindenburg Line.

The land in the region of Arras – Cambrai – St. Quentin saw some of the earliest and last fighting in the Great War. At each stage tactics, equipment and expectations were different; also different at each stage were the men who carried out the tasks of attack and defence. The changes in tactics and materials were due to experience and invention, the changes in men were due to the losses incurred at each stage. The names and dates of battles and actions fought during the war were formalised in 1921 by the Battles Nomenclature Committee. Use of this naming system allows the battles in the region to be set in chronological and geographical order.

The Battle of Le Cateau, 26 August 1914 saw the British falling back through St. Quentin, where they had established their General Headquarters when Le Cateau was threatened by the advancing Germans. Esnes was defended by the 2nd Royal Inniskilling Fusiliers with other units along the line to Le Cateau, which were to fall back later that day through Beaurevoir, Estrées and Villers Outréaux, villages which were later to be the rear areas of the Hindenburg Line. On 27 August many British troops poured into St. Quentin, all exhausted, having been marching and fighting for several days.

The 3rd Division had a brief pause at Bellicourt, where, four years later, the Americans and Australians were to have problems with the defences. This division, along with the 4th, then retreated through the villages which were to see British troops again in the following years. A number of rearguard skirmishes, mainly with German cavalry, were fought but the Germans were able to continue with their intended march to Paris. The towns and villages then became part of the rear under German occupation.

The autumn and winter of 1916 saw a resurgence of activity as the Germans began to turn the area into a defensive zone and the construction of the Hindenburg Line began. At this stage still well behind the front, as the Battle of the Somme was being fought some thirty kilometres to the west, the Germans began to upgrade railways and roads to cater for the material requirements of the engineers.

The German Retreat to the Hindenburg Line is officially classified as occurring between 14 March and 5 April 1917.

Although fighting in the area was in the latter part of this period, the Germans had been carrying out the *Alberich* operation of destruction of all amenities liable to be of use to the British who were closely following their retirement. As the Germans fell back onto the Hindenburg Line their rearguard actions often became more determined as they tried to hold onto the outpost zones.

The Battle of Arras, comprising a number of separate battles and actions in April and May 1917, saw the British trying to take the northern sector of the *Siegfriedstellung*. The attack was confined to the northern sector as this was the least affected by the withdrawal, which was of lesser depth between Arras and Croisilles. South of this the British were unable to build up the communications and transport systems in the devastated zone as quickly and were not in a position to begin an offensive. The morning of 9 April, 1917 – Easter Monday – saw the start of the Battle of Arras. The artillery bombardment had been started five days earlier, and had been designed to cut the barbed wire, destroy artillery batteries, and damage communications and transport; particular attention was given to known dug-outs and command posts. The bombardment was not continuous and many breaks were built into the schedule, one bombardment started at 5.25am to be followed five minutes later by the infantry and tanks. It was still dark, with snow clouds delaying the light of dawn, and the surprise timing of the infantry attack after the very short bombardment worked well; many Germans were unable to man their stations and were captured in their dugouts. The troops able to man their posts had the sleet blowing into their faces and this obscured their vision. In a few sectors the Germans managed to put up a fierce resistance but these were dealt with in some cases by tanks. The Germans were unable to call upon their artillery batteries for support as these were having their own problems; their guns and ammunition were blown up and the crews and horses of the batteries and supply columns were gassed. The gas used was lachrymatory, which was not lethal but prevented the carrying out of tasks. Lethal gas had been used in the earlier barrages, but it was not intended to make the area untenable for the new occupants, the British and Canadian infantry. Within a few hours the British had taken most of the forward part of the battle zone and were consolidating beyond the front trenches of the Hindenburg Line. By mid-morning the weather was improving and the German defence began to stiffen in some areas. The British troops pressed on and extended their penetration of the defensive zone.

Some German companies held out whilst surrounded, expecting

reinforcements to arrive at any time. Many of the German troops fell back, in accordance with their orders, to join the battalions they believed would launch a counter-attack and re-take the ground lost. It was intended that, if pressed hard, the troops in the forward zone would fall back and take up new positions on the intermediate line, the *Zwischenstellung*. Here they would be joined by reserves (*ablösung*) who would be stood-by, ready for action, ready to halt the attackers. In the event of the attackers not being halted, troops would again rally at the next line of defence. It was presumed that in this event the attackers would by now be exhausted and weakened by losses, and their lines of communication and supply would be stretched. They would therefore be unable to resist a concerted counter-attack against them. Five divisions of relief or counter-attack (*Eingriefdivision*) troops had been kept in reserve for precisely this situation. These fresh troops could then envelop the attackers and all ground lost would be regained. This was the plan, the first major trial of General Ludendorff's elastic defence. However this was not to come about because of German local commanders' failure – and refusal – to adopt the elastic defence system. Reserve troops and the counter-attack divisions were not close behind the rear line, ready to pounce, but many kilometres away, out of the range of artillery fire. So, the elastic defence scheme was not in place, and failed because it had not been properly applied. The British were able to take, fairly easily, most of their objectives, and at the end of the day considered themselves to be the victors. They were to prove unable to exploit the gains on the following day, 10 April, when British infantry spent the morning attacking positions which had been abandoned or were held by rearguard German troops. Cavalry was later used to try and press through the German lines, it had not been realised by the British planners that the Germans had pulled back to rear lines and there awaited the cavalry, which suffered large losses of men and horses before retreating. The second day of the Battle of Arras was therefore a disappointment after the previous day's successes. Realising that a good opportunity had been lost, on the next day, 11 April, the British decided to pursue what they thought was a defeated German force. Some success, such as the capture of Monchy village, was forthcoming, but the opening of the battle of Bullecourt was a failure.

The Germans had meanwhile been considering the reasons for the drastic defeat of 9 April and were taking steps to remedy these. Full authority to reorganise the defences was given to Colonel Fritz von Lossberg, who had hitherto disliked the method of elastic defence. Lossberg quickly visited all the battlefronts to assess the situation and develop the best defences. He considered that the British would need two or three days to bring up artillery for another assault and calculated that the furthest limit of British artillery fire was well in front of the main *Wotanstellung*. He therefore sited a new artillery defence line, the Rouvroy-Fresnes-Boiry Line, the *Boiry-Fresnes Riegel*, with a deep defensive zone in front of this. A rear defence line, *Wotan II Stellung*, was also started; it was accepted that the ground in some areas did not lend itself to rigid defence and some elasticity was warranted. Whilst this was being organised the British pressed on with their attack; an attempted thrust by the Essex and Newfoundlanders from Monchy-le-Preux became the first casualty of the new method of elasticity and counter-attack. Subsequent British attempts to reach the Drocourt-Quéant Line, via the fighting at Gavrelle, Roeux and Guémappe on 23 and 24 April, which became the Second Battle of the Scarpe, were very costly in casualties. Gains were limited as the Germans were not taken by surprise and their artillery was very effective. The revised system for the *Wotanstellung*, or Drocourt-Quéant Line, which was being perfected during the fighting, was similar to the earlier bringing forward of the first line of defence of the Hindenburg Line further south. The Rouvroy-Fresnes-Boiry Line was the first line of defence, with the ground in front of it covered by artillery. Behind this line was the battle zone, with many machine guns and strongpoints. Behind this zone waited the reserves, with transport to any particular sector, which would be able swiftly to re-capture any ground lost. The artillery was protected by the main Wotan Line. Thus what had been lines of trenches in echelon became a deep defensive zone. The Third Battle of the Scarpe, on 3-4 May, saw the British make another attempt to reach the Wotan Line; tactics were not matched to the defences and ended in total failure, with a very high casualty list. The few small gains which were made were soon lost to the counter-attacking Germans.

The disastrous results of 3-4 May were studied by the British: the liaison between tanks and infantry was determined to be critical, as was the timing of the initial artillery bombardment. A new sector was found where these ideas could be put into operation. The land south of the Arras battles was chosen as no major artillery operations had been carried out and the land was free of craters which would affect the tanks. The defences to be tackled were known to be the strongest the British had yet come up against – the fully completed *Siegfriedstellung*, the Hindenburg Line.

The Battle of Cambrai, November and December 1917, began with the concentration and assembly of troops, tanks and artillery in total secrecy, which was essential as it was known that the Hindenburg Line was relatively lightly manned, due to the fighting in Flanders. The artillery was not allowed to register its guns (scientific calculations of distance, map references, and weather conditions had been made) and tanks and troops were mustered in the dead of night. It had been calculated that the few main roads in the chosen area would soon be crowded and blocked, and possibly damaged, so the Royal Engineers made sure that their plans allowed for repair and replacement; forward transport would not be a problem.

At 6.10am on 20 November the planning came to fruition: all along the front tanks rolled across No Mans Land, with infantry following, as massed gun batteries in the rear – totalling just over 1,000 pieces of mixed calibre – roared into action and brought devastating fire down onto the German defences and batteries. Because of the known thickness of the barbed wire entanglements, and as the defenders' machine guns would probably be intact, the majority of the tanks were to be fully engaged in tackling the first objectives, the first lines of trenches and machine gun positions, alongside the infantry.

The opening of the offensive was a spectactular success, the Germans were taken by surprise and progress through the day fully justified the planning and the new tactics. With the exception of one sector, in front of Flesquières where the attacking infantry did not work well with the tanks, significant gains were made: many German prisoners and guns were in British hands and large breaches had been made in the strongest defences yet devised. More, smaller, gains, including the important position of Bourlon Wood on a high ridge, followed over the next few days but the initial impetus was soon lost: few reserves had been allocated to exploit the gains and press on through the *Siegfried II Stellung* and the *Siegfried II Zwischen Stellung*, the Masnières-Beaurevoir Line. The tanks, which had played such a major part, were withdrawn and the British soon found themselves back on the defensive. They then found that the Hindenburg system was yet to fulfil its second function, to act as a springboard for a counter-attack from behind the rear lines. The Germans considered that whilst they had given more ground than they wanted in the 'elastic defence in depth' the British advanced lines would be weak and their re-organisation of the former German lines would be incomplete. The counter-punch was launched on the morning of 30 November; the British were taken by surprise and lost most of their gains to date. A Court of Enquiry was held in January 1918 to determine the cause of the British failure to hold back the Germans. It concluded that troops were at fault for falling back in the face of superior attacking numbers and commanders could not, of course, be blamed for any mistakes.

Both sides had learnt a lot from the Battles of Arras and Cambrai and

The tank proved to be a very successful weapon during the attacks on the wire and trenches of the Hindenburg Line, especially where infantry liaison was good. The Germans saw the tank as a real threat to their defences and the morale of the troops and rapidly devised tactics and anti-tank defences. This included concrete and steel barricades, armour piercing guns and field artillery in tank forts. The tank in the top photo above, of C Battalion, attached to the 12th Division, whose emblem is seen, was knocked out on the edge of Lateau Wood on the first day of the Battle of Cambrai. It was also photographed by the Germans, middle photo, the lower photo is the site today, the D96.

were to use the experience in formulating future strategies. The British had been on the offensive all through 1916 and 1917 and all resources and doctrine had been concentrated on the principles of attack, with little thought given to defensive arrangements. Realising that they may soon be on the receiving end of a major German assault, thought was given to methods of defence during the winter of 1917/18.

The resultant organisation of the British defences was based upon the German system of defence in depth; the front and support trenches became the Forward Zone, with numerous machine guns and sufficient troops to repel an initial assault and delay a concerted attempt to break through. The Battle Zone was where the strongest defences and strongpoints, designed for all-round defence, were sited, and where it was expected most of the fighting would take place. The Rear Zone was sited as a rallying line should defenders be pushed back, and from here counter-attacks could be launched.

The organisers of the defences found that they had a mammoth task on their hands; such trenches as did exist, mainly the front line, were poorly sited, often marking the extent of an advance and frequently comprised earlier German trenches. Artillery and machine gun positions needed to be re-located and much shell proof accommodation had to be constructed for command, administration and accom-modation. The principles of the scheme were agreed in the middle of December 1917, and the British set to work. As most of the defence works were within artillery range of the Germans the great bulk of the task was carried out by the troops, with the infantry providing working parties. Work pushed on through the winter but progress was limited as labour and materials were not available in the quantities required. Initial emphasis was given to the Battle Zone; trenches were dug and wired and machine gun emplacements and dug-outs were constructed mainly by tunnelling. Very little use was made by the British of reinforced concrete for shell proof cover.

In the morning mists of 21 March 1918, the Germans left the trenches of the Hindenburg Line and swept towards the British defences. The major offensive, 'Operation Michael', which the British called 'the Offensive in Picardy' and 'the Battle of St. Quentin', had begun. German tactics had changed from earlier battles where all elements of the ground attacked were to be tackled. Specially trained Storm Troops (*Sturmtrupps*) were detailed to probe and infiltrate the British defences, leaving centres of resistance in the known strongpoints to be dealt with by troops following. Some of the strongpoints held out whilst surrounded but by the end of the day all of the Forward Zone and much of the Battle Zone had been lost. The battle

Easter 1918 and the Germans are once again in possession of the ruins of Monchy-le-Preux. The troops above are celebrating the day outside their shelter, the *Villa Rattenloch*. To the south the Germans had pressed the British back over the 1916 Somme battlefields but in this sector little ground had been gained.

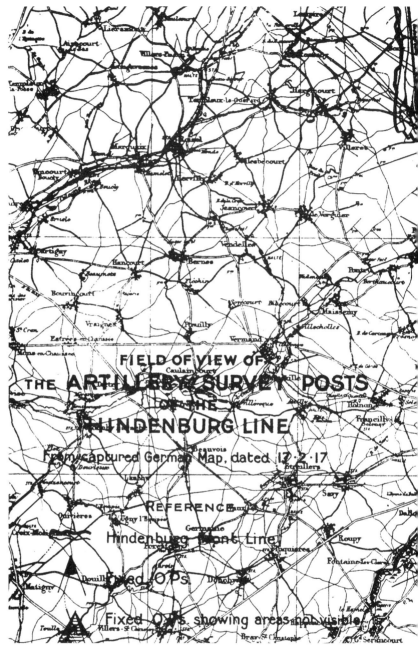

FIELD OF VIEW OF
THE ARTILLERY SURVEY POSTS
OF THE
HINDENBURG LINE
From captured German Map, dated 17·2·17

REFERENCE

Hindenburg Mont Line

Fixed O.Ps

Fixed O.Ps. showing areas not visible

An important aspect of the siting of the Hindenburg Line was the field of view over the British lines for German artillery observers. On first falling back behind the line, the Germans had complete command over the British lines so troop movements, transport and artillery batteries could all be watched. It was necessary for the British to change this situation; a German map was captured which showed the

44

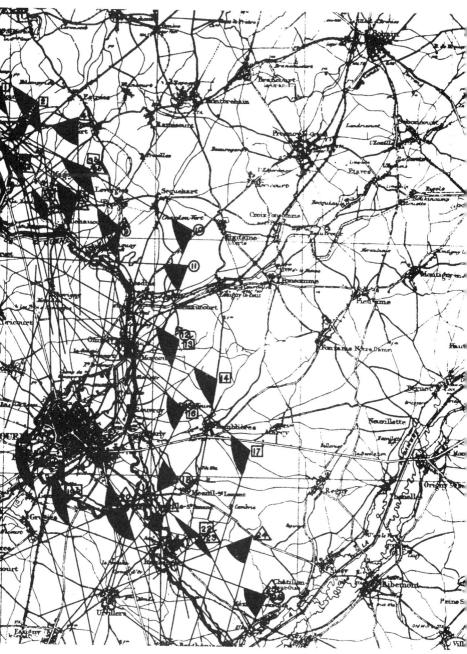

position of the observation posts and this made it possible to plan some counter measures, such as the concealment of positions, aerial bombardment and the use of smoke shells to hinder observation. The information contained in this map was used to help each assault on the German defence system.

45

passed away to the west as the German advance deepened and within two days the Hindenburg Line was once again in the quiet of the German rear zone.

Over the summer of 1918 the Germans abandoned the trenches and positions of the *Siegfriedstellung*, believing that they would not be used again. Trenches and dug-outs were unoccupied and neglected. At the northern end of the area things were different: The British were still in Arras and the Germans were still in the *Wotanstellung* or Drocourt-Quéant Line. The front lines were in much the same places as they were prior to the Battle of Arras. Between the Wotan Line and their front line the Germans had the *Boiryriegel*, and in front of this the *Monchyriegel* between Monchy-le-Preux and the British front was the outpost zone or *Vorpostenfeld* which ran from Neuville-Vitasse to Fampoux. This system of defence in depth was largely the result of the evolution of strategy during the 1917 fighting, although the giving of ground in elastic style did not feature in the defence tactics. The forward troops were not to retire in the event of a British attack but to stay and break up the waves of attack. The lines to the rear were stronger with many machine guns and field guns which would hold up the attack until the counter-attack or *Eingrief* troops arrived.

The system was put to the test during the Second Battles of Arras, beginning on 26 August. The Canadian and British divisions were aware that the attack was expected by the Germans but made good progress over the first lines. They were held up at the Fresnes-Rouvroy Line, the *Boiryriegel*, where many casualties were incurred. The Canadians managed to capture the line by attacking from Hendecourt-les-Cagnicourt, which had been taken by the British, and working northwards up the line. The Canadians were in no doubt about the formidable nature of the Drocourt-Quéant Line which they recorded as,

'one of the most powerful and well organised German defence systems. It consisted of a front and support line, both abundantly provided with concrete shelters and machine gun posts and protected by dense masses of barbed wire. In general the line was sited either on a crest or a forward slope in order to provide a good field of fire – the support system being on a reverse slope'[12]

This lay before them and had to be tackled. They decided to do this by concentrating the thrust on a small front, astride the Arras-Cambrai road, and then working to the south and north along the line. The Battle of Drocourt-Quéant began on 2 September 1918; the line was pierced on this day and the Canadians were planning to exploit their accomplishment the following day when they discovered that the Germans had abandoned the *Wotanstellung* as part of a larger retirement. They had fallen back to the *Wotan II Stellung* or Canal du Nord Line where they were to put up a spirited resistance.

The Battles of the Hindenburg Line began on 12 September 1918 as the Germans were being pushed back on to the defences which had been designed when their circumstances and tactics were different. They did not want the British to approach the main trenches of the Hindenburg Line and put greater emphasis on the defence of the Outpost Line. Schemes for the defence of this Outpost Line did not include elastic yielding but as the battles progressed this was inevitable; it was intended that any ground lost or given up voluntarily would be re-taken by the counter-attack troops but these were in very short supply as numbers of available troops diminished. The outpost zone was to be as wide as possible and only lightly manned, mainly by small groups of infantry and machine-guns in isolated posts. The main trenches in the battle zone were more strongly manned and also had numbers of tank forts, each with one or two field guns, machine-guns with armour piercing ammunition, trench mortars and searchlights. These were to prevent British tanks from pushing through the infantry lines to the artillery batteries behind. This Outpost Line included most of the former British front line from 1917 and was to deny the British further advance. To the rear the defences of the Hindenburg Line were hurriedly reorganised but still comprised the natural obstacle of the St. Quentin Canal with trenches on the eastern side. German maps of the Hindenburg Line defences, drawn up when they were in earlier use in 1917, had been captured by the British and the Germans were aware that their layout was no longer secret. The German re-shaping of the defences included strengthening around the natural 'bridge' over the canal where it went underground at Bellicourt and Bellenglise.

The Battles of Havrincourt on 12 September and Epéhy on 18 September, during which the Germans tried desperately to prevent the British from approaching the Hindenburg Line, resulted in the opposing lines being generally in the same positions they had occupied the previous winter. The British were now back in front of the Hindenburg Line and were to consider the best means and methods of tackling it.

From the ground the most obvious obstacle was the broad belts of barbed wire, much of which was well rusted, having been there for 18 months. Beyond the wire were trenches, concrete pill boxes for machine-gun and artillery positions, tank forts, tunnels and dug-outs for shelter, and numerous batteries of field and heavy artillery, with observation over the British positions and assembly areas. Beyond the Hindenburg Line the Germans were also bolstering the *Zwischenstellung* or Le Catelet Line and the *Siegfried II Stellung* or

Beaurevoir Line. In the event of these being captured the Germans had also begun work on the *Hermannstellung* I and II lines, some twenty kilometres to the east, near Le Cateau.

The British realised that the task before them was a difficult one; although the Germans had been pushed back involuntarily, and sometimes in disarray, the defences were the strongest ever constructed. The defenders may have had some morale problems and shortages of men but they were expected to resist penetration with vigour. The British planners had to find weakness in the system, and considered that the bridge at Bellicourt was a likely target. with a direct assault on the canal line. The attacks by the 46th Division, which crossed the canal, and the Americans and Australians at Bony and Bellenglise, spearheaded the assault and the *Siegfriedstellung* was broken.

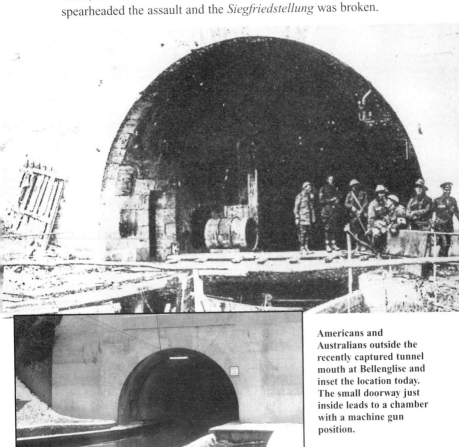

Americans and Australians outside the recently captured tunnel mouth at Bellenglise and inset the location today. The small doorway just inside leads to a chamber with a machine gun position.

CHAPTER FOUR

DRIVING THE HINDENBURG LINE

For this, the touring section, the Hindenburg Line has been divided into twenty parts for the convenience of the visitor. Clear maps provide routes, show the principal trench lines, and indicate remnants of the fortifications and of the Line still to be seen. The section between R and T has been omitted because it has no British connections (the French Army captured it in September-October 1918) and no traces or remnants exist today. Cemeteries, (British, French and German) are marked on the maps where they help with navigation or assist with the text. They do not include all British cemeteries.

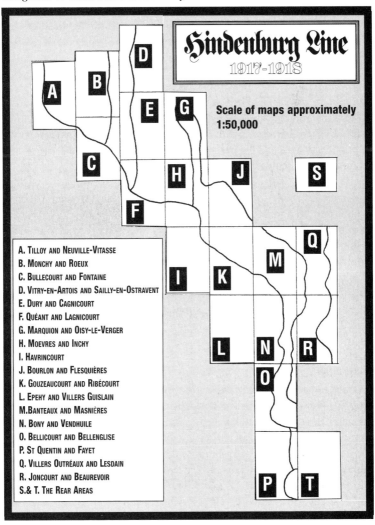

Hindenburg Line
1917-1918

Scale of maps approximately
1:50,000

A. TILLOY AND NEUVILLE-VITASSE
B. MONCHY AND ROEUX
C. BULLECOURT AND FONTAINE
D. VITRY-EN-ARTOIS AND SAILLY-EN-OSTRAVENT
E. DURY AND CAGNICOURT
F. QUÉANT AND LAGNICOURT
G. MARQUION AND OISY-LE-VERGER
H. MOEVRES AND INCHY
I. HAVRINCOURT
J. BOURLON AND FLESQUIÈRES
K. GOUZEAUCOURT AND RIBÉCOURT
L. EPEHY AND VILLERS GUISLAIN
M. BANTEAUX AND MASNIÈRES
N. BONY AND VENDHUILE
O. BELLICOURT AND BELLENGLISE
P. ST QUENTIN AND FAYET
Q. VILLERS OUTRÉAUX AND LESDAIN
R. JONCOURT AND BEAUREVOIR
S.& T. THE REAR AREAS

A

TILLOY AND NEUVILLE-VITASSE

Preparations for the 1917 British thrust from Arras had been exhaustive and detailed: ammunition was stockpiled, road mending materials dumped at strategic locations, light and standard gauge rail lines improved and made ready for jointing to the German system, and infantry objectives clearly defined.

Artillery bombardment began at dawn on 4 April, and for the next four days guns, ranging from 2inch trench mortars to 15inch rail mounted howitzers, pounded the German wire, trenches, roads, communications centres, ammunition depots and headquarters. Known and discovered German artillery batteries were to be bombarded for two days before the assault, with gas shells used for 10 hours before the infantry attack began.

Preparations had also been made to house and protect the troops prior to the attack; tunnels and caves beneath Arras had been extended and improved and bunks fitted. Together with the large cellars beneath the city which had been used to store merchandise and the sewer system, shelter was found for 24,500 men with communications centres and a hospital. Large dugouts were also dug at the front trench system, each sufficient to accommodate 2,400 men. Troops were therefore able to sit out the German bombardment (the Germans had been watching the build-up of troops and materials and expected an attack at any time, but did not know the planned length of the British bombardment) with a minimum of casualties. One battalion spent five days in these dugouts without a single casualty from the German retaliatory bombardment.

A raiding party of the 6th Queen's (Royal West Surrey Regiment) carried out a raid on the German trenches at 9pm on 7 April to ascertain the condition of the German trenches and check if they were still manned. Prisoners were taken for identification and it was found that the defences were very badly damaged.

Zero hour was to have been on the morning of 8 April, Easter Sunday; this day was sunny and clear but the start had been postponed for 24 hours at the request of the French who were to carry out their own attack further south. The assault began at 5.30am on Easter

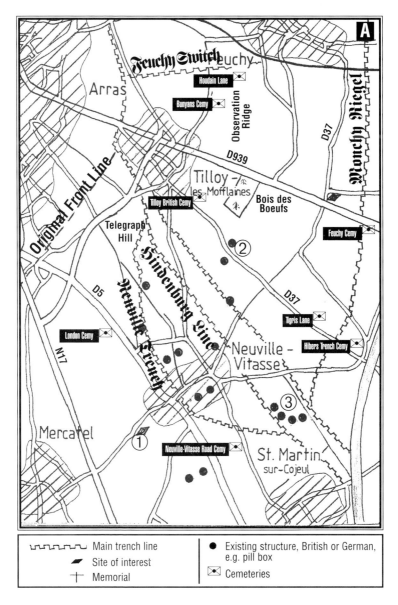

Legend:

- ⊔⊓⊔⊓ Main trench line
- ➤ Site of interest
- ✛ Memorial
- ● Existing structure, British or German, e.g. pill box
- ⊠ Cemeteries

Monday. The weather had deteriorated and snow was falling which hampered movement and assembling troops became soaked and chilled in slush filled trenches, although the snow was blowing from the west, into the Germans faces, which gave a distinct advantage to the attackers. The British troops of the 12th (Eastern) Division attacked the

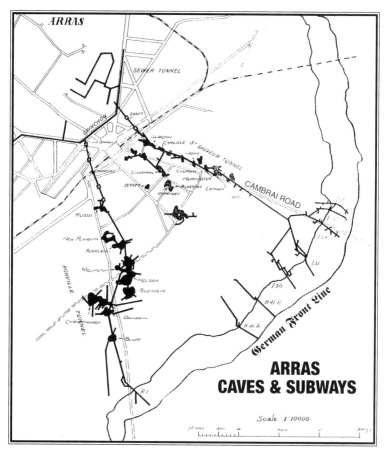

The caves and sewers under Arras were used to shelter troops before the attack began. Tunnels were dug which enabled them to emerge in No Mans Land. No British troops had had such protection before.

sector north of the Arras-Cambrai road, and emerged from the Arras caves into the front line. As this was expected to be a momentous and historical occasion arrangements had been made to film the event, but the camera operators were caught by gas from an exploding shell and the film was not made.

The Germans in the front line were taken by surprise and many were captured in their dugouts. The first objectives were taken easily but then resistance stiffened. The attackers had to take Observation Ridge which consisted of a series of strong points, wired trenches with machine guns. Two tanks were detailed to help, but only one arrived and the strongpoints were won by small teams using rifle grenades. One

52

Harry Cator

machine gun held up the advance in one sector until Sergeant Cator of the 7th East Surreys tackled it with a Lewis gun, killed the crew and the officer in charge, whose papers he then brought in. The attack was then able to continue and Sergeant Cator was awarded the VC. On the left Feuchy Switch trench also gave trouble but was overcome by the 8th Royal Fusiliers, who took 200 prisoners.

Some battalions had great success; the 5th Royal Berkshires found themselves facing four batteries of German field guns firing point blank at close range, rushed forward and captured twenty two guns with their crews, and then manned a couple of the guns and fired at the Germans. The 9th Essex made good ground and captured the strongpoint of Feuchy Chapel Redoubt which was in front of the last objective, the Wancourt-Feuchy Line or *Monchyriegel*. This last position was well defended with numerous machine guns and the advance ground to a halt in front of it. It was taken after a renewed atack on the following day.

The 3rd Division, on the south of the Arras-Cambrai road, also got off to a good start. Their objectives included the hinge of the Hindenburg Line, where it joined the original front line in front of Devils Wood, just west of Tilloy les Mofflaines, a strongpoint named the Harp to the south of the village and the Bois des Boeufs. It was intended to reach and take the Wancourt-Feuchy Line by the end of the day.

The 10th Welch Fusiliers entered Devils Wood and overwhelmed the occupants who put up little resistance. The garrison of Tilloy village, which had been strongly fortified, defended the village for some time before changing their minds when the 2nd Royal Scots and 7th Shropshire Light Infantry worked their way around them. The Shropshires then pressed on towards the end objective, capturing on the way several pill boxes where troublesome machine guns had sheltered, but were stopped in front of the defence line by machine guns.

Telegraph Hill gave the German defenders excellent views over the approaching British; the 10th Durham Light Infantry and 6th K.O.Y.L.I. suffered from the machine gunners on the Hill. Most of the German infantry waited in the dugouts, ready to surrender, but the stalwart machine gunners stayed at their positions until the British silenced them with Lewis guns and rifle grenades. Some of the posts held by the German machine gunners can still be found on Telegraph Hill.

Neuville Vitasse was a strongly fortified outpost of the Hindenburg

Line, with a main trench, Neuville Vitasse Trench, running through it, in front of this was Neuville Mill [**marked 1 on map**] which was a concrete blockhouse sited to prevent either frontal or flanking attacks on the village. The 1/3rd Londons of the 56th (London) Division cleared the blockhouse after a tank, specially detailed, had fired a shell through the machine gun aperture, killing and disabling the garrison. The Londons then continued to sweep through the village to the trenches of the Hindenburg Line, although the 8th Middlesex beside them were held up by an unsuspected machine gun post at the church. After stiff fighting the Middlesex took the position with 68 prisoners. Neuville Vitasse Trench was cleared by the 1st Londons after the Germans had caused the attackers many casualties. Although the main Hindenburg Line was taken after reinforcements came up progress was limited to the front trench (the 14th Londons, the London Scottish, had gone forward as far as the Tilloy-Wancourt road, where they captured machine guns, in two pill boxes [**no. 2 on map**], before falling back) as machine guns in pill boxes, which had also held up the 2nd Wiltshires and 19th Manchesters who were attacking from the front, across the track between St. Martin and Neuville Vitasse. These pill boxes prevented any further movement for the rest of the day so the 9th

One of the two concrete machine gun posts (the other can be seen to the left) captured by the 14th Londons (1st London Scottish) at the start of the Battle of Arras. The Scots had to retire from the position soon after capturing it.

One of the pill boxes taken by the Queen Victoria's Rifles after a strong German defence. The hungry Q.V.R's were pleased to also take the Germans' breakfasts.

Londons (Queen Victoria's Rifles) were instructed to clear them by bombing southwards down the Hindenburg Line from behind Neuville Vitasse. The Q.V.R.s had difficulty in reaching the start because of enemy shelling and their guide got lost, but once in position they started to work down the trenches and before long took the pill boxes, along with five German officers and 63 men of the 31st Regiment and four machine guns. They spent the rest of the day pressing further down the Hindenburg Line towards it's junction with the Wancourt-Feuchy Line. The Germans put up more resistance here and as by now light was fading the attack stopped and the Londoners consolidated their gains. They pressed again at first light on 11 April and with the aid of a tank bombed the Germans out of the trench junctions. The Germans were apparently not suspecting the early attack, and the Londoners who had not had supper or breakfast were pleased to find the defenders had left their breakfast behind:'some sliced sausage, black bread of very good quality and, most welcome of all, boiled eggs neatly packed in paper boxes.'[13]

The Q.V.R.s found also a number of machine guns and a good supply of ammunition, together with many grenades. They considered that it might be possible to extend their gains but, while signalling to the tank

which had assisted them, Lieutenant Smith was shot by a German sniper. Orders then came forward for them to join other battalions in a major assault on the Wancourt-Feuchy Line. This defence line had been the objective of the first day of the Battle and whilst some battalions held small stretches, it was still largely in German hands.

Feuchy, at the northern end of the Wancourt-Feuchy Line, had been cleared by the 7th King's Own Scottish Borderers after the village and its defenders had been given special treatment by a bombardment of 6 inch howitzers.

The approach to Feuchy had not been easy, Scottish battalions of the 15th Division had had to fight their way along the south face of the rail line which formed the south face of the Railway Triangle, a junction of main lines the embankments of which had been heavily fortified. The 9th Black Watch and other Scots worked through the triangle, bombing and bayoneting the

The German dug-outs provided protection from British shells. The infantryman above is enjoying a pipe but before long the British will be in possession of the shelter.

machine gunners after a tank, Lusitania, had fired 6 pound shells at them.

The battle then passed to the east, towards Monchy, and the former German front lines became billet areas for the British troops.

The following spring, 1918, found the area to be again hotly contested, and the Scotsmen of the 15th Division were once again in the thick of it. On 22 March the Division fell back onto the Wancourt-Feuchy Line, now the British front in the face of the massive German assault. A strongpoint was formed at the former German strongpoint of Feuchy Chapel, and the Germans tried to force the 13th Royal Scots from the position, which would have given them observation over Arras and would be a good start for an attack on the town.

The Royal Scots were determined to hold the line and defended it with all available resources and tenacity. Infantry losses were replaced with headquarters staff and the remnants held on, preventing a German breakthrough on the main road and killing many Germans who had reached as far as a Y.M.C.A. tent in the Bois des Boeufs. This position then became the hinge of the German 1918 advance, which was more successful to the south, Neuville Vitasse fell to the Germans but they could not move further and the western edge of the village became the front line.

The sector was held by the Canadians in August 1918. As a precursor to the main attack the 31st Canadian Battalion pushed the German 39th Division out of Neuville Vitasse on the evening of August 24. Two days later, at 3am on 26 August, the 2nd Canadian Division attacked south of the Arras-Cambrai road, with the 3rd Canadian Division north of the road. Although the Germans had prepared themselves for the attack resistance was not strong and the Canadians advanced rapidly.

THE AREA TODAY

Most of the caves beneath Arras are today closed to the public, those which are still in use and can be entered, such as the museum and the underground car park, are hardly recognisable as those which sheltered the British troops. Most were sealed after the war and remained inaccessible; these were entered in the winter of 1995/96 by two Frenchmen, Jannick Roy and Pascal Barrier who spent 63 days exploring the warren of tunnels.

The end of the Hindenburg Line, where it joined the original German front line, was by Devils Wood, which was cleared by the 10th Welch Fusiliers; on this ground now sits the buildings of the agricultural college. Some concrete remains of the Hindenburg Line can be found in the fields to the east of the town of Arras although most are slowly disappearing with the spread of the industrial area between Tilloy and the motorway. In recent years several pill boxes which formed the strongpoint of Feuchy Chapel were removed to make way for a new factory.

The high ground of Telegraph Hill contains some concrete vestiges of the German defences which were captured by the British. To the east, by the Tilloy-Wancourt road, are the remains of two concrete machine gun posts [no. 2 on map] taken by the 1st London Scottish on the first day of the Battle of Arras. Running through the centre of the nearby Bois de Boeufs is a now shallow German communication trench.

The defences of Neuville-Vitasse, the strong outpost village of the Hindenburg Line, contained many pill boxes and bunkers which had to be overcome by the Londoners who attacked the village and many of these still exist. The strongpoint of Neuville Mill was destroyed in later fighting, bushes on a piece of rough ground mark the site today.

On the front trench of the Hindenburg Line still stand the four pill boxes taken by the Queen Victoria's Rifles after determined German resistance [**no. 3 on map**].

Many of the strongpoints constructed as outer defences of the Hindenburg Line, well in front of the main trench, had to be captured before the main defences could be tackled by the British. This one, south of Neuville Vitasse, near the D5, was one of two mills which the Germans had fortified. The 2nd Wiltshires carried out an unsuccessful attack on the position during the night of 8 April and had to try again as part of the main attack on the morning of 9 April. They suffered many casualties before it was taken, after which many troops sheltered in the sunken Hénin-Neuville road, the D5.

B

MONCHY AND ROEUX

After the British had forced the Wancourt-Feuchy Line, troops were ordered to occupy Wancourt village by moving up the Cojeul valley, but this was easier said than done. The 7th King's Royal Rifle Corps advanced up the valley on 11 April but met a hail of machine gun fire, causing many casualties. However the Germans expected a repeat attack and decided to evacuate the village that evening. The buildings evacuated included a large concrete shell proof command bunker, which still stands on the edge of the village [**no. 4 on map**]

The large command bunker on the edge of Wancourt, with two chambers. The solidity of the construction is apparent, with hits from British artillery causing negligable damage. The earth breastwork shielding the entrance still remains, as does the earth camouflage on the roof. The other bunker nearby is not of the same quality, with thinner walls and a collapsed roof.

On the high ground to the east of Wancourt the Germans had a very good observation post, Wancourt Tower, an old windmill which had been strengthened with concrete to make it shell proof. This gave a good view from the southwest to the north, including the area now in British hands, enabling accurate artillery observation over the approaching troops, and close by was a concrete machine gun post which also poured fire into the attackers. The British realised that this position had to be captured or further progress would be difficult. The Tower was taken by the 1/6th Northumberland Fusiliers after a hard fight on 15 April; the Germans launched four counter-attacks that night to regain the position. They tried again the following night in heavy rain, and were successful so the Northumberlands tried to capture it again, this resulted in failure. The Germans retained observation over the British for another day. The Northumberlands were not to be denied and tried again on the morning of 17 April and this time they were able to hold the Tower – now in ruins – and consolidate the position.

David Philip Hirsch VC

After a period of stalemate, the British went on the offensive again on 23 April. The 30th and 50th Divisions were to move eastwards from the direction of Héninel and Wancourt.

The 4th East Yorkshires and the 4th Green Howards, of the 50th Division, reached the Cherisy-Guémappe road (the D38) where they came under heavy machine gun fire from Kestrel Copse by the road and were held up here. Captain D.P. Hirsch of the Green Howards tackled the machine gun but was then killed, being awarded the VC for his bravery. The new occupants were soon forced to

Kestrel Copse on the D38 where Captain Hirsch won his VC. In the copse are the remains of German steel shelters.

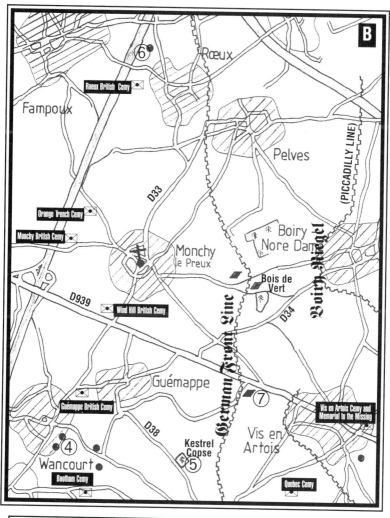

⊔⊓⊔⊓⊔⊓⊔ Main trench line	● Existing structure, British or German,
🢒 Site of interest	e.g. pill box
✝ Memorial	⊠ Cemeteries

hand back the copse in the face of a German counter attack as all battalions of the division fell back. The copse still stands **[no. 5 on map]** and the remains of two steel shelters can be found there.

The 30th Division was also having major problems. The 17th Manchesters and 2nd Royal Scots were cut to pieces by a German artillery barrage. The 8th Seaforth Highlanders, of the 15th Division, managed to push the Germans out of Guémappe village but only after several hours fighting and a high casualty list.

Monchy-le-Preux village sits atop a hill which gives good observation over the British lines to the west, and the German rear areas to the east, and both sides were determined to have it in their possession. The 13th King's Royal Rifle Corps and the 13th Rifle Brigade fought their way into the ruins on 11 April with the help of tanks which put out of action a number of machine guns. The 10th/11th Highland Light Infantry were entering from the north at the same time and the Germans were evicted. They then tried to shell the British back out with heavy artillery but the 4th Middlesex and 8th Lincolnshires entered as reinforcements and the village was consolidated. The 12th Division took over the ruins during the night of 11 April and cleared out the village cellars for shelter, handing them over to the battalions of the 29th Division on the following evening. Early on the morning of 14 April the 1st Essex and 1st Royal Newfoundlanders attacked out of Monchy to try and take Infantry Hill, Bois du Sart and Bois du Vert to the east; the attack began at 5.30am in the mist, the ground was wet and heavy from rain and snow but at 6.30am the attackers were in possession of their objectives.

The Germans had fallen back in an early exercise in the elastic defence system they had developed. Almost immediately the Germans counter-attacked and things began to go badly awry for the Essex and Newfoundlanders. First to suffer was X Company of the Essex, under Captain Foster who were overwhelmed at 7.30am then Z, Y and W Companies fell to the Germans. The Newfoundland Companies suffered likewise, A Company disappeared never to be seen again, C Company were known to have entered Bois du Vert but none returned to tell the tale. The two battalions had all but ceased to exist. The Essex began the attack with 923 men, of which they lost 661 killed, wounded or missing, (many were later known to have died of wounds as prisoners in Germany); the Newfoundlanders reported 487 casualties out of 591 men employed.

The defence of Monchy was then left to a small party of 10 men (mainly Newfoundland) who beat off an attempt by the 23rd Bavarian Regiment to retake the village.

Over the next months the front line was extended 500 metres to the east, almost to the crest of the high ground of The Mound (today marked by the modern water storage reservoir) on Infantry Hill. The opposing trenches were close, less than 100 metres apart in many places, and both sides carried out many trench raids to improve their positions. The 9th Royal Fusiliers recorded a raid by 100 men on 2

September, in which it took the troops, led by Captain Baudains, 30 seconds to reach the German line, where they destroyed dugouts and took 18 prisoners.

Defences were constructed in case of German attack; the Royal Engineers of the 12th Division built several shell proof shelters and artillery observation posts, sometimes using captured German materials. The 69th Field Company used a thick iron German observation post or *panzermebu* to form an observation post in the centre of the village, giving observation over the front lines and German battery positions. This now supports the Newfoundland Memorial.

The 15th (Scottish) Division held the village during the German 1918 spring offensive; the Scotsmen were confident that the line could be held but they were ordered to evacuate on the evening of 22 March due to the falling back of the division on their right.

Roeux, on the northern bank of the Scarpe, was another village which the Germans were determined to deny the British. A large scale attack by the 2nd Seaforth Highlanders and 1st Royal Irish Fusiliers on 11 April resulted in over a thousand casualties, mainly from concentrated machine guns around the chemical works by the railway station and the Chateau, where a large concrete bunker had been constructed. Two days later the South Africans tried to take the chemical works and other ruins but also were not successful. Scotsmen of the 51st Division managed to enter the ruins of the village and the chemical works during the major offensive on 23 April; for a short while they appeared to be in control but the Germans, some of whom were sheltering in limestone caves beneath the houses, pushed them back to their own front line. The story was the same for the 4th Division on 3 May: some success and penetration of the village defences followed by heavy casualties and no gains. This division had another try on 11 May, this time tactics were different - it was to be made in the evening so German information and communications would be hampered; it was hoped that the situation would be uncertain until morning. The attackers followed the artillery barrage into the chemical works and Chateau and took all their objectives. At the site of the Chateau the 1st Hampshires found the source of earlier problems, a large concrete machine gun post, with walls two metres thick and four machine guns. Some Germans still held out in the village and these were later cleared out by Scotsmen of the 51st Division. This Division was also to recapture the chemical works and village more than a year later, when on 26 August 1918 it wrested control of the ruins from the Germans.

The strong concrete bunker (no. 6 on map) in the grounds of Roeux Chateau housed several machine guns and provided the Germans with means to defend the village. It was found by the 1st Hampshires who cleared the immediate area, and taken again by the 51st Division in August, 1918. It was recently sealed to prevent entry.

On this day the Canadians were also very successful. Monchy-le-Preux was taken by the 1st and 5th Canadian Mounted Rifles and the 27th Canadian Battalion pushed through Wancourt, occupying the large German bunker there, and then worked up the hill to win Wancourt Tower. Two days later the Canadians captured Vis-en-Artois and the Rouvroy-Fresnes Line at Boiry-Notre-Dame. They then paused for a few days before pressing eastwards.

The Area Today

On the edge of Wancourt village are the two bunkers **no. 4 on map** by the Cojeul River and up the hill from here can be found the site of Wancourt Tower which was so important to the Germans.

By the side of the main Arras-Cambrai road is a small disused quarry, now partly filled, which formed part of the German front line after the battle of Arras **no. 7 on map**. Ernst Jünger, in *Storm of Steel* records being based in a dugout in this quarry in December, 1917:

'the gravel-pit was an unholy spot. Among the shell holes, filled with the refuse of war, the crosses of fallen trench-dwellers stuck up awry." [1]

Just south of Vis-en-Artois is the remains of an elephant steel dugout, probably dug and used by the Canadians as they planned their assault on the Drocourt-Queant Line. Of the many artillery observation posts constructed in Monchy village, only one – constructed in August, 1917 by the 69 Field Company, Royal Engineers, and utilising a German steel protective plate – still exists, atop this sits the Newfoundland Memorial.

To the east of Monchy-le-Preux is the low hill named Infantry Hill

The dugout near Vis-en-Artois, the hollows of others, long since collapsed, can also be seen in the small embankment, which provided natural cover from the Germans to the east. This was the Canadian front line prior to the assault on the Drocourt-Quéant line and was probably used as a medical aid post after the battle

which was the objective of the ill-fated Essex and Newfoundland attack on April 14, 1917. On the highest point, named The Knoll, now sits a modern water storage tank. The trees to the west mark the British front line, the German front line here was very close, 100 metres away, and the rough ground of their support with a section of communication trench can be found in the small copse by Bois du Vert.

The *Boiryriegel* defence line, named Piccadilly Trench (Fresnes-Rouvroy Line) by the British, was not reached in 1917 and held up the advance of the Canadians on 27 August 1918; machine guns of the German 141st Infantry Regiment from positions in Piccadilly Trench caused many Canadian casualties. The 52nd and 58th Canadian Battalions cleared these after hard fighting on the morning of 28 August, the pill boxes which were the scene of hand to hand fighting are still on the high ground, named Artillery Hill, north of Boiry-Notre-Dame. These can be found on the edge of the golf course.

The British observation post, constructed using a thick German steel sentry plate, beneath the Newfoundland memorial in Monchy-le-Preux.

C
BULLECOURT AND FONTAINE

The attack on Bullecourt was planned to assist the British as part of the Battle of Arras, it was expected that the Hindenburg Line here would be thinly held and a small offensive could push north eastwards and meet the main thrust behind the village. At Quéant, to the east, the Drocourt-Quéant Line (the *Wotanstellung*) joined the main Hindenburg Line and it was thought possible that the Germans might fall back to this position if attacked. The attack was allocated to the 4th Australian Division, who were to attack on the eastern side of Bullecourt, and the 62nd (West Riding) Division, who were to take the west of the village. The plan was for the attackers to by-pass the village, which would be heavily bombarded by artillery.

Planning got off to a poor start as heavy artillery and supplies could not get into position on schedule because of the packed roads, which were still not fully repaired following the efficient manner in which the retreating Germans had destroyed them. The first heavy shells fell in Bullecourt village on 20 March, disappointing the 121st Würtemburgers who had hoped for a quiet period after continuous fighting.

The main Arras battle began on 9 April, 1917. On the following day the attack on Bullecourt was to begin; the village was drenched with poison gas fired from Livens projectors and the thick belts of barbed wire were bombarded with high explosive shells fitted with a new type of instantaneous fuse (nicknamed 'ground shrapnel' and 'daisy cutters'). Zero hour was fixed for 4.30am; as the time approached the troops waited in a freezing snowfall for the tanks to arrive. The Australians had not seen tanks before and were not sure just what to expect. The tanks did not arrive, having had difficulty finding their way from Noreuil in the snow, and, as the troops huddled in their front line positions poised to go over the top, the decision to abandon the attack was made. As the troops began to withdraw from their attack positions the light grew and it was feared that the Germans would see them and bring down artillery fire but fortunately snow began to fall again and obscured them from German eyes. The message cancelling the attack did not reach all of the units; the 2/7th and 2/8th West Yorkshires did

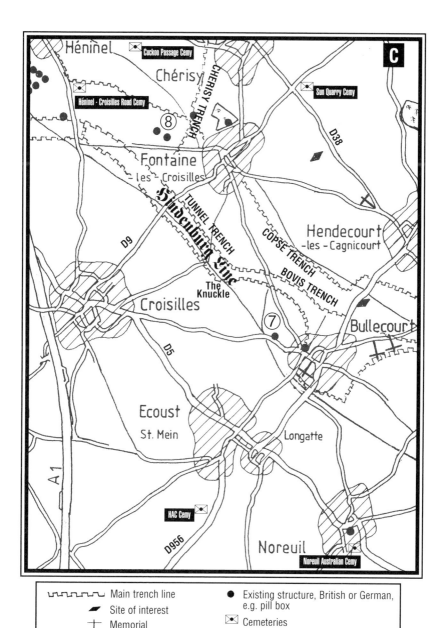

ᴸᴸᴸᴸᴸᴸᴸᴸ Main trench line	● Existing structure, British or German, e.g. pill box
◣ Site of interest	
┼ Memorial	⊠ Cemeteries

not receive the information and, unaided by artillery and expecting the Australians to be along side them, they went forward as planned. Forward patrols reached the first German defences and breached them before realising that they were on their own and after suffering 162 casualties they withdrew to their own lines.

On the following day, 11 April, despite Australian objections, the attack began again. The eleven tanks, by now arrived and refuelled and with the crews rested, went forward to open up gaps in the wire and, with the infantry following, to encircle Bullecourt village. The tanks were of limited success as being very visible against the snow covered ground they were an easy target for the German gunners, some were stationary because of mechanical problems and, whilst firing on machine guns, were put out of action one by one. Accounts of the ground made by the tanks vary, a report of two tanks entering Riencourt and Hendecourt are disputed by Australian infantry and by the Germans. The majority of the tanks did not get across the Hindenburg Line, and only one is known to have reached Bullecourt. Few gaps were made in the barbed wire belts and the infantry were left to subdue machine guns themselves. Despite this the Australians managed to occupy the main Hindenburg Line trenches after hand to hand fighting and tried to consolidate them for further advances.

Early reports were received at British headquarters that Bullecourt had been captured, so the cavalry - the Sialcot Brigade - were sent forward to pass through the village. The reports were not correct and the cavalry suffered losses before it reached the railway at the British front line turned back.

Two small lengths of German trench lines, between Bullecourt and Riencourt, were occupied by the Australians.

Artillery support was not given because of incorrect reports of the extent of the advance and then the Germans counter attacked from within Bullecourt and from the eastern flank. German machine gun fire from many posts prevented movement over open ground and fighting was confined to bombing with grenades along the trenches. The Mills Bomb hand grenades were more effective than the German egg-bombs although these could be thrown further. The Australians were able to hold off the German counter attack until they became desperately short of grenades. Machine gun fire prevented any ammunition or reinforcements getting across from the British lines so the Germans were able to close in along the trenches, working from bay to bay. By 12.30am the fight was over, those Australians who could not escape from the Hindenburg Line were killed or taken prisoner.

Many wounded of both sides lay around the battlefield and then occurred the rare event of an informal truce whilst stretcher parties collected the dying. At 6pm the truce ended when snow began to fall, neither side trusting the other in limited visibility. Over the next few days wounded, who had been lying out in shell holes, crept into the

British lines; as late as the night of 15 April – four days after the battle – Privates Carne and Ryan, of the 47th Australian Brigade, who had been in a shell hole beyond the German wire, returned.

Australian losses were very high, especially for 4 Brigade, which was almost destroyed, having some 2,339 casualties out of 3,000 troops in action. The Australians were particularly galled by the number who, out of ammunition and surrounded, were forced to surrender – the Germans took 28 officers and 1,142 men prisoner. The disaster was blamed on the tanks, which had not lived up to the promised expectations. The Germans recorded their defence and counter attack as a great success, seemingly particularly pleased that the nightmare of tanks had been removed and their defence methods proven.

The Germans suspected that the British would have another attempt to take Bullecourt and organised a pre-emptive strike. At 4am on 15 April they swept out of the Hindenburg Line and met with varying degrees of resistance. They had taken the Australians by surprise and took some forward posts, fighting their way almost to Noreuil before being stopped by tough resistance. Lagnicourt to the south east fell but before long the Germans were driven back to their Hindenburg Line defences.

Plans and arrangements for a second attack on Bullecourt were made over the next few weeks, and the 62nd Division and the 2nd Australian Division made themselves ready. One aspect of the plan was a very heavy artillery bombardment of Bullecourt, Hendecourt and Riencourt. Heavy guns were drafted in from other sectors of the front including many batteries of 60 pounders and 6 inch and 9.2 inch howitzers, with some 12 and 15 inch howitzers. These began a systematic destruction of the three villages, all known German batteries, defences, trenches and wire. On 20 April the last buildings in Bullecourt was destroyed. Throughout the heavy bombardment, which continued for two weeks, the German defenders were safely below ground in shell proof bunkers and dugouts in and around Bullecourt. Some were large and spacious, holding up to 80 men, where the garrison 'sat in its dugouts, and, in spite of the shells and trench mortar bombs, preserved its freshness.'[15]

The date set for the attack was changed several times. It eventually began at 3.45am on 3 May; the Australians from New South Wales and Victoria were to pierce the Hindenburg Line between Bullecourt and Riencourt, then capture Hendecourt, whilst the West Yorkshiremen on their left were to take Bullecourt village and the defences west of it.

The Australians immediately ran into problems. On reaching the barbed wire of the German front line in front of Riencourt in the dark (it was not yet dawn) the New South Welshmen came under heavy machine gun fire and sheltered in shell craters, before falling back in confusion and disarray. The order to retire was given by an unnamed Australian officer who panicked[16].

On the east side of Bullecourt the Victorians, who started out from the railway line, fared a little better before running into real trouble. As they reached the wire they came under fire from a machine gun which was silenced by Lewis gunners firing from the hip as they advanced. The first two German trenches were crossed but they then found that the trenches on their right were still in German hands. The fighting was now largely along the communication and main trenches of the Hindenburg Line. Progress was halted where the Bullecourt-Riencourt road crossed the main trench, this was the same position where the Australians had been stopped in the earlier battle on 11 April. This is the site of the Australian Memorial. The Germans had a large stock of grenades and showered these on the Australians who, under Lieutenants Thwaites, Braithwaite and Jennings, threw Mills grenades in return and slowly made headway, capturing two bays, losing one, capturing two more, again losing one to the Germans who then made a stubborn stand until a Stokes mortar under Lance-Corporal Mitchell arrived and helped drive the Germans back. The position was then rushed by a party under Sergeant Arblaster and Corporal O'Neill. Fighting continued all day with little more progress being made. The Six Cross Roads was reached by the 24th Battalion under Captain Maxfield, who captured Ostrich Avenue, called *Cannstatter Graben* by the Germans.

The British on the left had also had problems achieving their objectives. The 2/5th West Yorkshires managed to cross the front line and enter Bullecourt village, where they formed a strongpoint at the church and then reached the northern outskirts before being pushed back by the Württemburgers. Three tanks went into the village but liasion with the infantry was poor and no advantage was made. One tank was hit and set on fire and the other two also suffered damage. On the northern side of Bullecourt a party of the 2/7th Duke of Wellington's and 2/8th West Yorkshire Regiments reached their objective near a sugar factory (the site is still evident) before being surrounded and cut off in a German trench. The party of two officers and 31 men were spotted by an air patrol at 7.15pm, at 6.15am the following morning (4 May) they were seen by another air patrol but were never seen again. It was presumed that they were afterwards either captured or killed.

Reinforcements were desperately needed if Bullecourt was to be taken, so battalions of the 7th Division were ordered to try again at 10.30pm. Plans were hurried and did not allow full reconnaissance of the ground. The Welch Fusiliers and Honourable Artillery Company reached the first line, Tower Trench, and passed on into the village before being thrust out by the Germans. Repeated attacks were ordered over the following days, most met with a little success with ground won being retaken by the defenders. By 15 May the area around the church was held by 20th and 21st Manchesters when a major German effort to recapture this part of the village, by now merely rubble, was launched. Some ground was lost by the Manchesters who then regained it. On 17 May another British attack, this time by the 2/5th Londons (Rifle Brigade) and 2/8th Londons (Post Office Rifles) coincided with a German retreat from the village to the northern outskirts. The Londoners pressed them back and occupied the main defence trench named Bovis Trench. They were unable to penetrate further and so this became the front line until the following March.

The tired 7th Division and 1st, 2nd, 4th and 5th Australian Divisions were withdrawn for rest. Casualties were about 14,000 on the British side, with similar losses for the Germans.

The Hindenburg Line to the northwest, where the Germans had repulsed the 62nd Division, was still wanted by the British. The section of front trench named The Knuckle, as it kinked due east here, was raided by the 2/1st Battalion London Regiment, with a detachment of 504 Field Company Royal Engineers at 11.30pm on 8 June. Second Lieutenants Selden and Ward, with a party of 58 men were to gain

The forward battle headquarters dugout as it is today of the West Yorkshires and other Battalions of the 62nd Division used during the fighting for Bullecourt. It was dug during the battle by the 457th (West Riding) Field Company Royal Engineers.

information on the defences, take prisoners for interrogation, and destroy some concrete machine gun positions which had been causing trouble. The raid was a success; 20 Germans were killed, valuable information gained and one prisoner – an Alsatian from Strasbourg, of the 99th Regiment - captured, who was communicative and gave further details of the German defences. One raider, Corporal Thornhill, became temporarily separated from his group and found the entrance to a very deep dugout, which confirmed the length of Tunnel Trench.

Battalions of the 7th Division, now officially rested and refitted, took over this sector in mid June and continued to harrass the Germans. The German front line contained a number of concrete machine gun emplacements, named Og, Gog, Magog, Mars, Jupiter, Juno, Neptune, Mercury and Vulcan, which prevented any further advance although some were captured in local operations and raids. Some changed hands several times: Gog and Magog, in the German front line, were found to be unoccupied by a patrol of the 2nd Queen's (Royal West Surrey Regiment) under Second Lieutenant Short on the night of 14 June, although these were later lost again.

Tunnel Trench was about 10 metres beneath the surface and was about four kilometres in length, running from The Knuckle along the front Hindenburg Line in a northwesterly direction to where the high ground between Fontaine-les-Croisilles and Héninel sloped down to the latter village. Some sections of the tunnel were in British hands and some were held by the Germans, who blew the roof in as a stop. Two metres wide and 2.5 high, when fully occupied it held between 2,000 and 3,000 troops. Many battalions had their headquarters in the tunnel along with various officers and stores. To maintain order a Town Major, Second-Lieutenant W.B. Drake of the 10th Essex, was appointed. Siegfried Sassoon described taking the 50 steps down to the Tunnel, 'that triumph of Teutonic military engineering with its earthy smell and deathly cold winds'.[17]

While they were based in the Tunnel, the 10th Essex, under Second-Lieutenant R.H. Binney, patrolled into the part of Tunnel Trench held by the Germans, and found the sentries were asleep, as were more Germans in a small shelter. These were then 'winkled out' and taken prisoner.

The section of Tunnel Trench and the tunnel between The Knuckle and Fontaine-les-Croisilles was attacked by battalions of the 16th (Irish) Division on 20 November as a subsidiary to the main battle of Cambrai.

The objectives included some concrete emplacements as well as trenches and the Tunnel; 6th Connaught Rangers took Jove and Mars

German engineers bringing up materials for the Hindenburg Line defences to the south of Héninel, on the road towards Croisilles, and the same scene today (lower).

from the rear, establishing Company headquarters in them, but soon the Germans launched a concerted counter-attack and re-took Jove, killing many of the Irishmen and Lieutenant Smith of the Royal Engineers who had stood on top. Tunnelling Companies, 174th and 262nd, had accompanied the infantry to take and consolidate the Tunnel, losing some parties of sappers killed on the way, some by the accidental detonation of their own explosives. The Engineers had a reasonable idea of what to expect in the Tunnel as they had interrogated a German from the garrison, the 471st I.R., who had surrendered the day before. Many Germans were captured in the Tunnel, which was found to be wired for demolition. In one section a German Major showed the location of 27 mines, mainly two trench mortar shells wired with detonators.

Héninel Hill, the high ground between Fontaine and Héninel, was the objective of the 21st Division on Easter Monday, 9 April 1917. The

German defences here were effective and were well utilised by the garrison; the attackers managed to reach the front trench of the Hindenburg Line but the foothold was tenuous and very many losses were incurred. The Germans tried to dislodge the British from their gains; a counter-attack on the following day, 10 April, pushed the 21st Division out of the Hindenburg Line on the slopes of the hill. Both parties used many grenades and Private Waller of 10th Kings Own Yorkshire Light Infantry was awarded a posthumous VC for holding back the Germans with grenades.

Horace Waller VC

The 18th Manchesters won their objective of the Hindenburg Line section on the high ground during the morning of 12 April. Second Lieutenant G.S. Martin crossed the Sensée River before dawn to locate the forward positions of the Germans. A Company, under 2nd Lieutenant S.M. Shirley, then crossed the river at 3.00am and bombed their way into the German trenches; the defenders - the 220 Infantry Regiment - were called upon to surrender but did not so were either killed or fled. The area between the crest and Héninel village, where they met the Queen Victoria's Rifles, was cleared by C Company, under 2nd Lieutenants B.A. Westphal and J.E. Smart, reinforced by D Company. The Manchesters found in addition to the concrete machine gun emplacements a number of deep dugouts, connected by continuous passages over 400 metres in length. In two dugouts were 12 wounded men of the 21st Division, captured the previous day:

'they had been bandaged and given food and drink by their captors. Many Germans were having a meal of hot coffee, after fighting, our men regaled themselves with hot drinks, Lager beer, eggs and tinned food. In one dugout, 50 loaves found'.[18]

Losses were light, six killed and 27 wounded although not all units were so lucky: the 5/6th Scottish Rifles and the 1st Cameronians of the 33rd Division suffered several hundreds of casualties on 13 April and on the following day the Queen Victoria's Rifles (56th Division), in an attempt to take Chérisy from Héninel village, lost 361 men, including five Lieutenants; Blackwood, How, Gibb, Bartman and Saxby.

The Hindenburg front line from Héninel southeastwards as far as a block at Fredrick Lane was now British; down to and past Fontaine-les-Croisilles remained in German hands. On 23 April a major attack was launched by the 33rd Division, the objective was to bomb along the trench and enter Fontaine from the northwest while a simultaneous attempt to enter was made from the west, along the Sensée valley. A small advance along the Hindenburg Line was made but this was limited and the frontal attack was not successful, Fontaine was to remain in German hands.

THE AREA TODAY

Bullecourt shows little evidence of the intense fighting which levelled the village in 1917. The site of the sugar factory where the party of the 2/7th Duke of Wellington's West Ridings and 2/8th West Yorkshires held out and then disappeared can be found by the D956 and the roof of one of the German bunkers can be found in the village. The fields to the south and east were where much of the fighting occurred, the Australian memorial marks the limit of their advance. The railway embankment which formed the British front line and shielded troops from the Germans is now disused and overgrown.

In Noreuil is a large British concrete bunker built to protect heavy artillery which pounded the Hindenburg Line and targets to the rear during the winter of 1917/18, and helped the 2/5th Sherwood Foresters defend the village for a few hours on the morning of 21 March 1918, before falling to the Germans. It was recaptured in late August of that year.

One of the many dugouts in which the British sheltered, made plans and tended wounded during the fighting for Bullecourt still exists **no. 7 on map**. Between Bullecourt and Fontaine-les-Croisilles ran the Hindenburg Line with the Tunnel underground. This was closed after the War and is slowly collapsing, evidenced by deep craters which occasionally suddenly occur along its length. The many pill boxes – Juno, Jupiter, Mars etc. – which gave so much trouble to the British opposite The Knuckle, have long since been removed and the fields are bare of any remains.

North of Bullecourt, just by the D38 Hendecourt-Chérisy road, is a

Noreuil, an outpost village in front of the Hindenburg Line, was captured on 2 April, 1917 by the 50th Australian Battalion. The village was defended by the 119th Reserve Infantry Regiment, who were initially taken by surprise but then put up stiff resistance, killing many Australians before ceding the cluster of houses. The British then organised the defences in the village, which became part of the Battle Zone. This included a Siege Battery of the Royal Garrison Artillery, and a concrete bunker was constructed inside a cottage for these heavy guns in September 1917, probably by 132 Army Troops Company of the Royal Engineers. The emplacement was sited to fire over the ruins of the church, the two chambers for the guns were named Little Joe and Big Ben. The design included the use of a false roof and air space to minimise the effects of a shell hitting the construction. The photo *above and right* shows a Canadian officer on the roof, after it was recaptured at the end of August 1918, watching the Germans who were again settling into the Hindenburg Line a few kilometres to the east, whilst a British Tommy cleans a captured German Maxim 08/15 machine gun. The sheets are improvised gas curtains. *Right*: the same bunker today.

short length of German trench, part of *Hendecourt riegel*, called Ulster Trench by the British. The trench, marked by a number of trees in a field, is about two metres deep but appears to be getting shorter each year with agricultural operations around it.

In Fontaine-les-Croisilles the site of the large German rail sidings and engineers stores where most of the materials for construction of the Hindenburg Line were off loaded is now occupied by the village football field. Nearby, on the edge of the wood, is a large artillery bunker with several chambers and showing signs of small arms fire from when it was captured by the 52nd Division on 27 August 1918. To the west of this village are two concrete machine gun posts [**no. 8 on map**], these were sited on Farmers Lane, a communication trench. Another, which can be entered in dry weather, is by the track to the northeast.

On the high ground of Héninel Hill, south of Héninel, is a cluster of dugout entrances and *doppelmebus* or armoured double machine gun posts, these are those cleared by the 18th Manchesters and found to contain British wounded.

One of the cluster of bunkers to be found on Héninel Hill. This was one of the entrances to the underground shelters dug into the hill, the strong concrete protected the dugout entrance and also contained a sheltered observation post which gave good views over the British positions. British Battalions were to make good use of the dugouts during the later fighting on the hill; on 26 April 1917 the 19th Manchesters had their HQ here.

D

VITRY-EN-ARTOIS AND SAILLY-EN-OSTRAVENT

The village of Vitry-en-Artois was an important position on the Drocourt-Quéant Line (*Wotanstellung*) – with high ground to the south, Mt. Metier and Mt. St. George, it covered the approaches along the Scarpe and the flatter land to the north. Strong defences had been built in 1916 and early in 1917 these were strengthened in case the British – pressing out from Arras in April – penetrated this far. The defences were again strengthened in the summer and autumn of 1918, although limited resources meant that many positions were not finished by the time the British attacked. The German planners wished to prevent an attack along the line and into Douai, to the northeast, thereby threatening vital rail and industrial interests.

Sailly-en-Ostravent, south of Vitry, was important as a junction of the *Wotanstellung* and the Sailly-Arleux Switch Line. Following the British advance in late August 1918 – the Battle of the Scarpe – the Germans had been pressed further eastwards, sometimes retiring and sometimes putting up strong resistance.

On 7 October, at dawn, the British 8th Division had tackled the Rouvroy-Fresnes Line: by 8am the 2nd Middlesex had captured Biache St. Vaast; The Germans put up limited resistance and then retired further east to the safety of the *Wotanstellung*.

A full attack by the 8th Division, with the 1st Canadian Division on their right, was planned for the morning of 11 October. The 8th Division were to storm the *Wotanstellung* and pass through Vitry, taking all the land on the north of the Scarpe, the Canadians were to take the high ground south of the river, Sailly, and the land either side of the River Sensée.

The Germans, in anticipation of the assault, had largely withdrawn from the line, but had left rearguards with many machine guns in strategic positions. The 8th Division advanced rapidly, capturing the defenders of Vitry and the town by 9.30am but were unable to advance further: the Canadians had not been able to capture Mt. Metier and machine guns on this high ground, in addition to preventing forward progress by the Canadians (15th Canadian Battalion, the 48th Highlanders of Canada), were sweeping the ground north of the river and holding up the troops there. The Canadian H.Q. acknowledged that the British were being held up by their failure to take Mt. Metier, reporting that "the 23rd Imperials" (the 23rd Brigade) on the left were in Vitry.

At 13.13pm a platoon of the 48th Highlanders of Canada, under Lt. G. Davies, went forward along the south side of the river to try and take the machine guns which were causing the hold-ups.

The 8th Division troops – the 2nd Middlesex – who were held up in Vitry, realised the cause of the problem and decided to act. At 4pm a platoon of the 2nd Middlesex – led by Brigadier General Grogan (who had earlier won the Victoria Cross, for gallantry during the Battle of the Aisne in May 1918), and the battalion commander, Lieutenant-Colonel Baker – crossed the Scarpe by the ruins of the railway bridge and attacked the machine gun posts on Mt. Metier, capturing the hill from the flank. Another platoon of the 2nd Middlesex crossed the Scarpe and took Mt. St. George, silencing the machine guns there. Both operations were considered a success, with low casualties – three other ranks wounded. At 5.20pm the Canadians reported that their objectives had been taken and they had overcome the resistance of five machine guns. The report, and subsequent records, did not mention the 'Imperials' or the 2nd Middlesex. Mt. Metier still contains, in the sand pit there, the defences which were fought over on 11 October 1918. The 16th

One of the pill boxes in the sand pit on top of Mt. Metier. This gave good views over the attackers, holding off the Canadians until the 2nd Middlesex took it by crossing the Scarpe and coming from the direction of Vitry. The same pattern of steelwork can be found at other locations, such as Lormisset Farm, near Beaurevoir, and Monchy-le-Preux.
Several other posts and bunkers are at the same site, one displays the use of British steel girders.

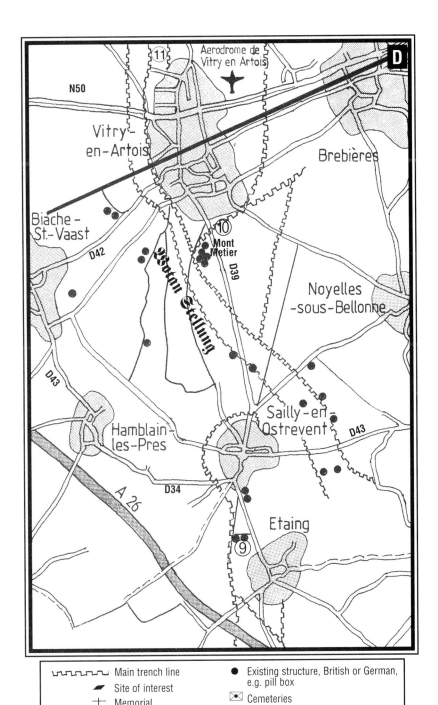

Main trench line
Site of interest
Memorial
Existing structure, British or German,
e.g. pill box
Cemeteries

Canadian Battalion, the Canadian Scottish, had meanwhile attacked the village of Sailly-en-Ostravent and the *Wotanstellung* there. They found no opposition until the front line had been crossed, and there were no Germans in the village. They reported that there was 'no sign of 15th Battalion on left', who were still held up by the high ground. They then came under machine gun and rifle fire from rising ground to the northeast, Mont Notre Dame. Lieutenant Stevens, with the 3rd Canadian Trench Mortar Battery, attacked the position, driving the garrison into dugouts with Stokes shells and then took the Germans – 18 from the 140th and 358th Regiments – prisoner. By the late afternoon, all of the objectives of the attack on 11 October - several villages and a length of the *Wotanstellung* – had been taken.

VITRY AND SAILLY TODAY

Many of the permanent defences constructed by the Germans and captured by the Canadians and 2nd Middlesex still exist and can easily be found today.

To the west of the D39, south of Sailly, is a pair of large reinforced

This large German bunker was sited to guard against any attack along the Canal. Built on the inside of a house which stood here, the impression of the door can be seen. This fell to the 2nd Middlesex on 7 October, 1918; they encountered little opposition and suffered very few casualties.

German bunkers – probably a forward HQ for the infantry regiment which held this sector, the 358th Regiment. This bunker [**no. 9 on map**] was abandoned by the Germans on being attacked by the Canadian Scottish. On the other side of the D39, close to the road, is a partly finished bunker, part of the defences which were still being upgraded in October 1918. The construction shows several chambers and the typical layout of an infantry or artillery command post.

The Arleux Line joined the main Drocourt-Quéant Line (*Wotanstellung*) on the north side of Sailly and from here the Canadian Scottish came under fire. Concrete dugouts which featured in this action can still be visited in the fields by the Noyelles-sous-Bellone road, the D39, although only the roofs of some are visible.

Mt. Metier – indicated by the water tower – was the site of the strong point which held up the Highlanders of Canada; in and around the sand pit are the remains of the defences which the Canadians and the Middlesex fought over. On the northern edge of the pit – adjacent to the track – is a reinforced concrete observation and machine gun post with a thick steel lining of a pattern which can be found at various sections of the Hindenburg Line (*Siegfriedstellung*), this is also of the same type as that re-used by the British for the construction of a concrete observation post which now sits beneath the Newfoundland Memorial in Monchy-le-Preux. In the centre of the sand pit are several concrete bunkers, which have been dislodged by later sand extraction. Also here is the single wall of a field gun emplacement. Three iron girders jut out from the top of the wall and one of the girders clearly shows where the beam was produced:

'MADE IN ENGLAND', another gives more information:
'CARGO FLEET ENGLAND'. Cargo Fleet was a steelworks near Middlesborough.

It is quite possible that the cement used by the Germans is also of British origin. The inset steel protective plates show obvious damage of small arms fire, although some of this may be from later in the Second World War when the position became important again [**no. 10 on map**].

The view from the northern face of the hill, over Vitry and the Scarpe, and that from the western face, over the land the Canadian Scottish had to cover to approach the position, gives an appreciation of the importance of the site.

Between the Scarpe and the N50 is the village of Vitry-en-Artois, taken by the 2nd Middlesex who were then held up there by machine gun fire from Mt. Metier. North of the N50 the defences of the *Wotanstellung* had been assaulted and taken by the 2nd Devonshires on 11 October: these defences were later incorporated into the defences

The Germans were not able to complete all of their planned defences and some concrete constructions were unfinished such as this bunker at Sailly-en-Ostravent. The shape and wall thickness show typical layouts of many such constructions.

of the airport when this was constructed by the Germans in the early 1940's. A concrete and brick underground shelter [**no. 11 on map**] is on the line of the *Wotanstellung* Reserve line and a revolving steel gun emplacement, on the rising ground to the west, is on the site of a 1918 emplacement.

Much of the soldiers' accommodation was in strong shell proof shelters; these Germans in a bunker with three three tiers of bunks have made space for a writing table, complete with a vase of flowers.

E

DURY AND CAGNICOURT

An important part of the Drocourt-Quéant Line or *Wotanstellung* was the high ground, named Mont Dury, which overlooked the approaches along the Arras-Cambrai road. This had been strongly fortified by the Germans, as had Etaing to the north and Cagnicourt to the south. This sector was one of the most powerful and well organised German defence systems with several lines of trenches and many machine gun and artillery positions.

The British and Canadians had spent the latter part of August 1918 pushing the Germans back to this defence line; on 30 August the 1st Rifle Brigade and 1st Somerset Light Infantry of the 4th Division entered Eterpigny after several attempts, and on the same day Hendecourt was taken by the 57th Division and the Canadians took a number of strongpoints and outposts in front of the line. Plans were then made for a concerted assault on the defence line on 2 September.

The line between Dury and Etaing was the responsibility of the 4th Division. On the night of 1 September Mark V tanks were taken forward to within 300 metres from the German front line. To drown their engine noise the R.A.F. flew twin-engined aircraft over the trenches although the infantry were still worried that the Germans would hear them and be forewarned of the attack. The night was dry but clouds increased the darkness, and at 5.00am the troops went forward and the attack began. The 1st Rifle Brigade attacked out of the ruins of Eterpigny and took its first objective, the first trench of the Drocourt-Quéant Line, without difficulty but were then held up by machine guns which were extremely accurate and caused many casualties. They pushed on and found two batteries of 77mm field guns firing at point blank range. During the battle for these guns two company commanders were taken prisoner by the Germans but later escaped. The guns, and controlling artillery bunker **no. 13 on map** were eventually won and the Rifle Brigade moved on to the next line before being stopped by heavy machine gun fire. On their left the 2nd Essex and 1st Somerset Light Infantry also started well, taking the first and second trenches with little difficulty but were then halted by withering machine gun fire which kept them pinned down for several hours.

The 2nd Lancashire Fusiliers had been in support for the attack but came forward and joined in. Almost immediately an officer, Captain Bowen, was killed by artillery. Second Lieutenant D. McIntosh and his runner, Private Currie, saw two field guns which were causing casualties and had crippled one tank, so the Lancastrians rushed the guns, killing an officer and three men at one gun; at the other gun the artillery officer was loading the gun when Private Currie shot him and took prisoner the crew.

Several of the machine guns holding up the advance were positioned in and around Prospect Farm, others were sited on the high ground to the southeast of Etaing, in the concrete pill box which still stands there (**no. 12 on map**). These machine guns needed to be silenced before any further progress could be made and the 1st King's Own went forward to carry out the task, capturing the guns and the farm.

During this time the 38th and 85th Canadian Battalions had fought their way through the wire and over the trenches of the Drocourt-Quéant line and took the crest of Mont Dury; from here they were exposed to a storm of fire from machine guns in the sunken road which runs between Dury and Villers. These were tackled and cleared with the assistance of tanks and as the Canadians could make no further headway the sunken road became the front line. The 46th Canadians fought through the ruins of Dury village through which ran the support line; several strongpoints were taken with 120 prisoners and nine machine guns.

South of the main road initial opposition was light, the Germans being taken by surprise. The 14th Canadians swept into Cagnicourt and captured the garrison of several hundred who were still in the village cellars; the defenders in Villers-les-Cagnicourt and the Buissy Switch line in front of the village were more alert and the 10th Canadians suffered heavily from machine guns and trench mortars. It was 11pm before the Canadians had secured the village.

The day of 2 September 1918 had been a difficult one, the British 4th Division and the Canadian Corps had smashed this section of the Drocourt-Quéant Line but could not pass further because of determined opposition from the Germans. Five Canadians and one American, Lance-Corporal Metcalfe, MM, who was serving with the 16th Canadian Battalion, were awarded the VC for actions during the day.

William Henry Metcalf VC (American)

Plans were made for the advance to continue on the following day, 3 September, but air patrols at dawn found that the Germans had fallen back to the Canal-du-Nord Line to the east. Some rear guards

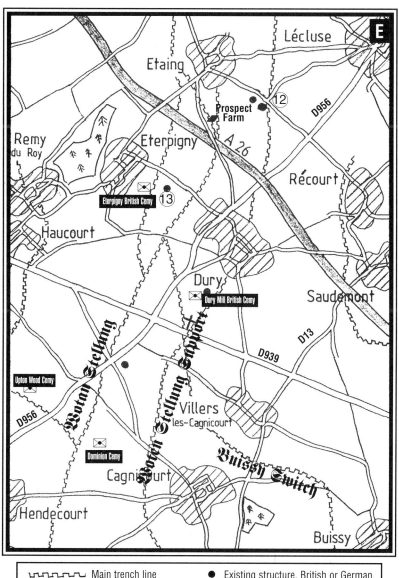

ꙍꙍꙍꙍ Main trench line	● Existing structure, British or German, e.g. pill box
◣ Site of interest	
✝ Memorial	⊠ Cemeteries

had been left to slow the British advance but many of these were half-hearted; two Officers of the 1st Somerset Light Infantry – Captain Lester and Lieutenant Dickinson – walked alone into Lecluse where 25 rear guard Germans surrendered to them. The 2nd Essex and 2nd Lancashire Fusiliers went into Etaing village but met little resistance. The Canadians went from Dury into Recourt and Saudemont, which were empty.

THE AREA TODAY

The marshes to the north of Etaing formed part of the defences of the *Wotanstellung*, being guarded by the road to Sailly-en-Ostravent which was a causeway. Prospect Farm, from which machine guns halted the British advance, was not rebuilt after the war but the site, and the commanding view (now partly obscured by the motorway embankment), is still evident. To the southeast of Etaing, on the D39, is the pill box which also caused problems [**no. 12 on map**]. About 100 metres away is the concrete roof of a command post, often only identifiable by a patch of coarse grass. The road from Eterpigny to Dury crosses the Drocourt-Quéant Line, where the 1st Rifle Brigade attacked on 2 September. The command post of the artillery which fired at them over open sights can still be found close by, although its original trench level means that it now stands about 250cm high [**no. 13 on map**]. On the crest of Mont Dury is the military cemetery; about 100 metres north, still on the crest, is the roof of an observation post, now earth covered.

F

QUÉANT AND LAGNICOURT

This was a very important sector of the Hindenburg defence system, where the main Hindenburg Line or *Siegfriedstellung* met with the Drocourt-Quéant Line or *Wotanstellung*. The original siting of the *Siegfriedstellung* was behind Quéant and Pronville but a later adjustment added outworks which became part of the main system and brought the forward line, named the *Balkonstellung* (Balcony Trench, on account of its jutting out) in front of the villages.

In March 1917 the Germans were falling back to these defences but were putting up a stubborn refusal to be pushed right back to the line and intended maintaining outlying villages as outpost zones. Lagnicourt was to be defended to prevent the British approaching too close to the *Siegfriedstellung* and was garrisoned by the 91st R.I. Regiment, part of the 2nd Guard Reserve Division. The 26th (Queensland and Tasmania) Battalion was ordered to capture the village; the plan was for one Company to press through the centre while one Company swept around the left of the village and one took the right side. Before dawn, in drizzling rain, the infantry followed the artillery barrage towards Lagnicourt. The right Company, under Lieutenant Lloyd, worked their way around the east of the village, putting out a German searchlight which had impeded them, and reached the northeast houses, where they captured several German medics. The left Company, under Captain Cooper, also encircled the village, where they awaited the emergence of the centre Company, meanwhile shooting Germans, including the garrison commander, who were fleeing the village towards Quéant. The centre Company, under Captain Cherry, had met with stiff resistance, being fired on from windows and doors of houses and barns. The first major check was cleared by Private C. Nutt, firing his Lewis machine gun from the hip. More fights followed and made progress along the main street slow; two hours behind schedule they reached the meeting place at the northern end of the village. The northeastern outskirts then became the Australian front line and defences were hurriedly organised. A German counter-attack followed swiftly, the attackers, of 119 Reserve Infantry Regiment, pressed the Australians back into the village before falling back themselves when

Percy Herbert Cherry VC

the impetus petered out. Heavy shelling continued; one shell killed Captain Cherry, who was awarded the VC for his part in working his way up the main street, and other officers who had resisted the counter-attack.

The Germans made another determined attempt to re-capture Lagnicourt a few weeks later, on 15 April. Infantry from four divisions with storm battalions and engineers, a total of 16,000 troops, were ordered to take Lagnicourt and the British line down to Boursies and press on past Morchies. The attackers managed to penetrate the Australian defences in the ruins of Lagnicourt, taking prisoners and destroying some artillery pieces in gun batteries before being forced back to the Hindenburg Line by the Australians.

The section of the British line facing Quéant then became relatively quiet, the battles of Bullecourt and Arras were fought off to the northwest, Riencourt-les-Cagnicourt was an objective during Bullecourt but the Hindenburg line was not breached here. On 20 November 1917, Quéant was bombarded with gas drums as a diversionary attack for the start of the Battle of Cambrai which was fought off to the east and south, with the left flank of the attackers, the 56th (London) Division starting from Boursies. Quéant was again left to its defenders.

The full thrust of the German spring offensive, on 21 March, 1918, fell upon the 6th Division: the Germans managed easily to overcome the British front line but were then stopped in their tracks by a determined defence which resulted in high casualties on both sides. Several more attacks followed, the Germans probed and infiltrated the British defences but with many of their own losses. After gaining a foothold in the British front line the Germans worked sideways down the line and widened their gains. Slowly the British were pushed back past Morchies.

In late August, 1918 the Germans were again falling back towards the strong defences of Quéant, with the Scotsmen of the 52nd (Lowland) Division pressing eastwards along the front Hindenburg Line, rolling the defence line up. The defences in front of Quéant were considered to be impregnable without a major tank attack, these were not available in sufficient numbers so the 57th Division, following the Canadians who had breached the Drocourt-Quéant Line (*Wotanstellung*) just north of Riencourt-les-Cagnicourt, then swung south and fought down to enter Quéant and Proville from the northwest.

In Quéant, between Abbey Farm and the church, was found a large concrete emplacement for a heavy gun, with rail connection for

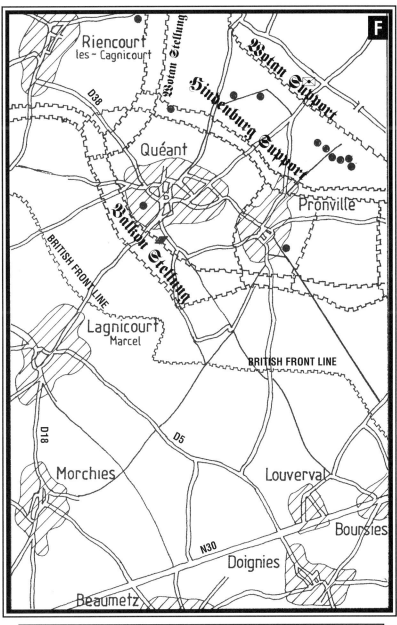

F

Riencourt
les – Cagnicourt

Wotan Stellung

Wotan Support

Hindenburg Support

D38

Quéant

Pronville

BRITISH FRONT LINE

Balkon Stellung

Lagnicourt
Marcel

BRITISH FRONT LINE

D18

D5

Morchies

Louverval

Boursies

N30

Doignies

Beaumetz

	Main trench line	●	Existing structure, British or German, e.g. pill box
⬛	Site of interest	⊠	Cemeteries
✚	Memorial		

The bunker which housed the heavy German gun that fired on the British during the Battles of Arras, Bullecourt, Cambrai, the 1918 spring offensive, and covered the retreat to the Hindenburg Line. Quéant was a very strongly defended village at the junction of the Hindenburg and Drocourt-Quéant lines, the British were unable to take it in 1917 but forced the Germans out in 1918, after which Field Companies of the Royal Engineers lived here.

ammunition, which had been active during the battles of Arras, Bullecourt and the German spring offensive. It had also been used recently. The emplacement became home to the Royal Engineers of the 52nd (Lowland) Division who took over the following day. The Engineers recorded their tenancy with an inscription on an inside wall:

412 LOW. FIELD COY R.E. 3.9.18

The 57th Division were billeted in the village when they returned for a rest; their Engineers from Wessex also used the emplacement and recorded their stay:

502 WX. FIELD COY R.E. 15.9.18

THE AREA TODAY

The concrete gun emplacement in Quéant [**no. 14 on map**] still stands and still contains the Engineers inscriptions. It can be found at the far corner of the sports field behind the village church. The trench gauge railway embankment for the ammunition supply can still be discerned, as can the ammunition hatch, which had a fixed loading crane, in the roof. In the high bank of the sunken road leading south out of Quéant were the battalion headquarters of the German units which held the front of the Hindenburg Line and from where attacks were launched. These dugouts, tunnelled into the bank and sited so as to be shell proof, are now collapsed but can be identified.

The construction to the south of Pronville is from the Second World War, part of a military airfield which was here. The cluster of bunkers to the north of Pronville, from where machine guns held up the British advance, were cleared by Drake Battalion of the 63rd Division during the late afternoon of 2 September 1918.

The area of the Hindenburg Line has not had the same attention of tourists and visitors as other British sectors of the Western Front, it is therefore much more easy to find debris and souvenirs, such as this German helmet recently found in a wood. The rusted area is around a shrapnel or shell shard hole which probably killed the wearer.

G
MARQUION AND OISY-LE-VERGER

After the British, with the Canadian Corps, pressed the Germans back from the Drocourt-Quéant Line or *Wotanstellung* on 2 September 1918, Hindenburg considered the area between that defence line and the Canal du Nord to be difficult to defend and, at noon on that day, ordered a withdrawal to the Canal du Nord Line. This line ran along the eastern edge of the canal, which along this section was filled. The natural marshes alongside much of its length, which had been flooded by the Germans, made a major obstacle, with good views and clear fields of fire over the land to the west of the canal. Running almost parallel with the Canal du Nord line, about a kilometre to the east, they had constructed another major defence line, the Marquion Line or *Fafnerriegel* which ran down from Oisy-le-Verger, behind Marquion to Bourlon Wood.

As the Germans fell back to the Canal du Nord Line on the night of 2/3 September the Canadians continued to press them, taking Baralle as the defenders left. This had been an important administrative centre with many headquarters and offices; on the marshland between the village and the Canal du Nord were railway sidings and stores areas. Rumaucourt and Lécluse were also occupied after being evacuated. For the next three weeks the Canadians and British consolidated their defences and made plans to cross the canal and force the defences on the eastern bank before tackling the Marquion Line defences. The natural obstacles of the canal and the flooded marshes in front of the German defences prevented a direct frontal attack; the plan was to cross where the canal was dry (at Inchy, to the south of Baralle) and spread out northwards through Marquion, Sauchy Lestrée and Sauchy Cauchy to Oisy-le-Verger. The 1st Canadian Division, with the 11th (Northern) and 56th (London) Divisions were to carry out the task in the early morning of 27 September.

The attack started with Canadian artillery, which had been brought up during the night, firing point-blank at the enemy positions on the far side of the canal. Between Baralle and Marquion the canal held five

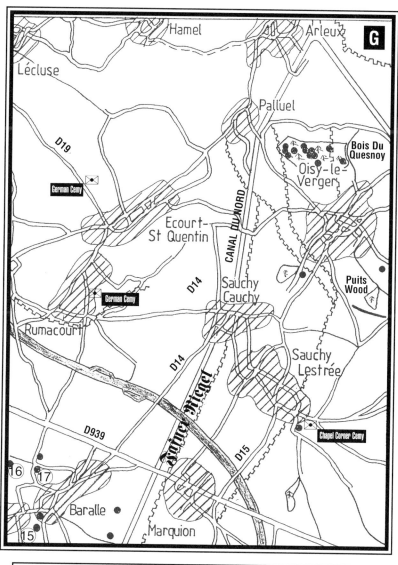

Main trench line

Site of interest

Memorial

● Existing structure, British or German, e.g. pill box

Cemeteries

metres depth of water and the 11th Manchesters crossed, on bridges thrown across by the Royal Engineers, as the left flank of the attack. The Manchesters and 15th Canadian Battalion surged into Marquion

One of the command bunkers which are still to be found in Baralle, (numbered 15 on map).

In the centre of Baralle village is a light signal post and telephone centre which had lines to the gun batteries and infantry command stations.

and the assault on the Marquion Line followed. Field Artillery crossed the canal to assist, and the advance pressed northeastwards, past the German defence line and towards Puits Wood. The 11th Manchesters had led the assault but had to stop at the railway cutting by Puits Wood, the 8th Northumberland Fusiliers continued and captured Oisy-le-Verger with 200 prisoners.

The 56th (London) Division had meanwhile tried to cross the canal to the north of the Arras-Cambrai road (the D939), approximately where the motorway now crosses. They were delayed by Germans on the east bank who prevented the construction of trestle bridges by the Royal Engineers. After two hours the passages were in full use and the infantry crossed and fought their way northwards along the Canal du Nord and Marquion Lines. Sauchy Lestrée and Sauchy Cauchy villages were taken together with the woods and copses around them, and the Londoners then went on to meet the Northumberland Fusiliers in Oisy-le-Verger before tackling the Bois de Quesnoy, which was very heavily defended as it allowed views over the open ground and another German defence line, the Brunemont Line, to the north.

In the quarry on the outskirts of Baralle is a large bunker, with many chambers, which was being constructed when the Battle of Cambrai started. The engineers soon had other priorities as the British approached, work was abandoned but the attackers did not get this far, being held up at Bourlon Wood.

THE AREA TODAY

In and around Baralle village are many of the bunkers and shelters which the Germans constructed as part of the permanent defences. The quarry, which is now being slowly filled in, has several large bunkers, one of which [**no. 16 on map**] was half completed; the concrete is only half way up the elephant steel shelters forming the five chambers and gives a good indication of the wall thickness. A command post is nearby, in the corner of the walled enclosure [**no. 17 on map**]. A telephone centre and light signal post (*Blinkstelle*) still stands high in the village centre and 150 metres down the street is another concrete command post, another nearby larger one was recently demolished. On the site of the former rail sidings and stores near the canal is a large concrete bunker and an observation post with steel lining is nearby.

On the outskirts of Sauchy Lestrée is a large concrete command post, probably for the 186th Regiment which held the Marquion Line (*Fafnerriegel*) which ran through the village, still inside the ruins of the farm (Ferme de Sauchicourt) which concealed it. This post was captured by the 11th Manchesters on 27 September. The Bois du Quesnoy, a strong position guarding the end of the two defence lines, still holds twelve concrete machine gun posts, shell proof shelters and command posts. Several have been dislodged due to recent sand extraction, which still continues and the wood and sand pit are private property where access is generally not allowed.

German bunker, part of the rail sidings which were between Barralle and the canal.

MOEVRES AND INCHY

Demicourt was on the left of the 36th (Ulster) Division, with Hermies on it's right the Division launched an attack on the Hindenburg Line in November 1917 to coincide with the capture of Havrincourt by the 62nd Division. After a short but intense artillery barrage the 10th Inniskillings rushed the first objective, a spoil heap on the west bank of the canal. The garrison, from the 20th Landwehr Division, did not fight. Most fled up their own trenches. After this puncturing of the defences the 9th Inniskillings then took up the fight, working northwards up the dry bed of the canal and the trenches of the Hindenburg system with rifle grenade and bayonet, clearing dugouts as they were captured. Resistance had stiffened by the time the 11th Inniskillings relieved their colleagues but by 3.30pm they had reached the main Bapaume-Cambrai road; more Inniskillings were sent forward with the 14th Royal Irish Rifles to take Moevres. Fighting was now desperate, and continued into the following day, 21 November, when German machine guns and artillery halted the Ulster advance. The outskirts of Moevres was entered but the German positions here were very strong and the gains could not be held, the village remaining in German hands.

The command bunker on Canal Trench was captured by Ulstermen and became a front line post for the 13th Essex and 2nd South Staffords when the Germans held the canal lock. The insignia plaque of the German regiment which was over the doorway has been removed. The interior door frame shows improvisation by the builders, the use of a bed frame (no. 21 on map).

This large and strongly reinforced concrete pill box on the southern edge of Inchy prevented the British from capturing the Hindenburg Line beyond Tadpole Copse. Built into the first house of the village, (the brickwork texture is still evident) it had an extensive field of fire over the attacking Londoners of the 56th Division and commanded the ground they hoped to take. It was captured by the 63rd Division during the final offensive, on 3 September 1918.

The attack was repeated the following day, 22 November. At 11am the Ulstermen stormed the village and by late in the day had reached the northern houses; a strong German counter-attack pushed them back and they ended up in their starting positions. Meanwhile the 56th (London) Division were attempting to take the Hindenburg Line to the southwest of Moevres and the small wood named Tadpole Copse, which lay on the front of the defensive zone and was strongly defended. The wood and trenches were heavily bombarded before the Queen's Westminster Rifles wrested the Germans from their positions. Tadpole Copse was held as a front line post by the Londoners until 30 November, when the London Scottish were ousted by a major German attack.

The German view of the counter-attack against the British in this section of the Hindenburg Line is given by Ernst Jünger in *Storm of Steel*[19]. Jünger describes the nature of the fighting in the trenches; much bombing from traverse to traverse with both sides losing men and ground in repeated attacks and counter-attacks, with machine guns taking heavy tolls. His unit, the 73rd Hanoverian Regiment, was attached to the 225th Reserve Regiment which was attacking the 2nd

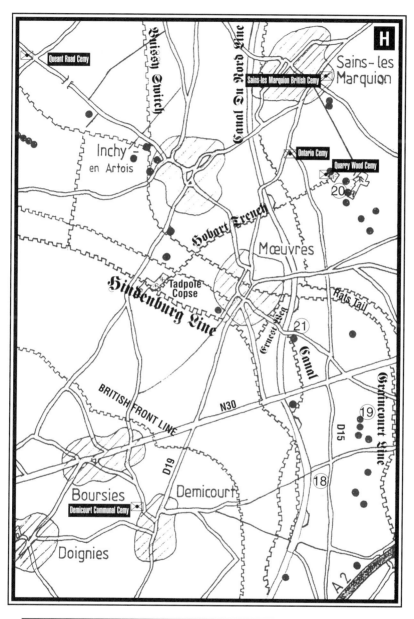

Map legend:

- ꟼꟼꟼꟼꟼ Main trench line
- ◣ Site of interest
- ✛ Memorial
- ● Existing structure, British or German, e.g. pill box
- ⌧ Cemeteries

Map labels: Queant Road Cemy, Buissy Switch, Canal Du Nord Line, Sains-les Marquion British Cemy, Sains-les Marquion, Ontario Cemy, Quarry Wood Cemy, Inchy en Artois, Hobart Trench, Mœuvres, Rats Tail, Tadpole Copse, Hindenburg Line, Ernest's Seq, Canal, Graincourt Line, BRITISH FRONT LINE, N30, D15, D19, Boursies, Demicourt, Demicourt Communal Cemy, Doignies, A2

This German command bunker, built into the lee of a road embankment, was an important centre of activity whilst the Germans were preventing the British from taking Inchy during the opening stage of the Battle of Cambrai. It was lived in by a French family until the early 1990's, after it was abandoned the doors and windows were bricked in.

and 56th British Divisions. Lock 5 and the area around the existing concrete bunker, (**no. 21 on map**) were held by B Company, 13th Essex, under Captain F.R. Keeble. The 99th Machine Gun Company had several machine guns sited around the lock, and with these and rifle fire they beat off a determined assault by the Germans until they ran short of ammunition and grenades. At 10.20am a heavy barrage of gas shells and heavy artillery preceded another attack and the Essex were forced to evacuate the lock and fall back to the trench beside the bunker, Canal Trench. The Germans immediately occupied the lock; B Company together with some of A Company under Captain H.H. Duff and the 2nd South Staffords (under Second Lieutenant C.T. Hindle), having replenished their supplies of ammunition and bombs, tried to force the Germans back from the lock but after hand-to-hand fighting the Germans remained there with the 13th Essex at the bunker and in Canal Trench.

Other units were also under great pressure. The 17th Royal Fusiliers were holding a trench named the Rats Tail when they were forced to retire by the weight of the German attack. A rearguard defence by troops under Captain Stone and Lieutenant Benzecry held the attackers back for a while, but after desperate fighting the defenders fell one by one. Lieutenant Benzecry was last seen wounded in the head but fighting until he fell dead, Captain Stone was then shot dead, and none of the troops of the rearguard survived. Captain Stone was posthumously awarded the Victoria Cross

The Hindenburg Line between *Donner Weg* and *Ernst Weg* communication trenches, opposite Moevres, was held by the 17th Middlesex and the 1st King's Regiment, with the front line in the Hindenburg support line. B Company of the King's, under Lieutenant Taggart, was practically annihilated with a few survivors withdrawing down *Donner Weg* where Sergeant Woods and his men managed to stop the Germans with bombs and hold up their advance here. A concerted effort was made by the attacking Germans to bomb their way down *Edda Weg*; a bombing party of the 1st King's comprising Sergeant Gannon and five men held them back for a while but most of the party were. Another party succeeded in forcing the attackers to a halt and Edda Weg remained in joint tenancy. *Ernst Weg* was defended by C Company of the King's, after several hours fighting along the trench only a small party of a dozen troops under Second Lieutenant Scott remained alive, who managed to halt the advance before being pushed back to the main trench.

Walter Napleton Stone VC

Fighting along the trenches continued throughout the day and evening. Early the following morning, at 4.45am on 1 December, the Germans tried again to capture the Hindenburg Line; after losing many men they reformed and attacked again at 9am. Some progress was made down *Edda Weg* until a counter attack by Captain A.M.C. McReady Diarmid and some of D Company of the 17th Middlesex Regiment. With a plentiful supply of bombs – all thrown by the officer – the party re-took 300 metres of *Edda Weg*, and 67 dead and 27 wounded Germans were attributed to the officer who was awarded the Victoria Cross for this feat.

Allastair Malcolm Cluny McReady Diarmid VC

Sections of the trench system had changed hands several times over the two days fighting and both sides had lost very many men. The result was that the British retained some of the Hindenburg Line and the Germans had some, with stops in some trenches separating the two sides. The Germans considered themselves fairly successful for despite their heavy losses, especially of officers, they had been on the offensive against the British for the first time since the middle of 1915, moreover they had learnt a lot about penetrating defences and were to hone this information over the next months while planning their spring offensive. They were even more pleased to find that, between 4 and 6 December, the British had pulled back from their positions in the Hindenburg Line and withdrawn to a prepared defensive line in front of Boursies and Demicourt, where they were to spend the winter awaiting the expected spring offensive.

The attack of 21 March 1918 came not from the east but from the north. After soaking the area in gas for twenty four hours the Germans pushed back the 17th and 51st Divisions, clearing Demicourt and Boursies in an attempt to close the Flesquières salient from behind.

Later in the summer the Germans were again on the defensive and were pushed to their defences of the Hindenburg Line by the Grenadier Guards who took Boursies on the afternoon of 3 September; on the same day the 17th Royal Fusiliers swept through Doignies, facing little opposition, but were stopped once they reached Demicourt.

The next stage – crossing the Canal du Nord – took some planning and it was 12 September before the attack was launched. The Highland Light Infantry stormed the canal in front of Moevres at first light and crossed with little difficulty; the Ox and Bucks, who were to cross directly opposite Demicourt, were less lucky and were swept by machine guns on the eastern bank. Fighting continued throughout the day and into the night, in pitch black and heavy rain the Ox and Bucks made repeated attempts but were finally forced to accept that, for the time being, they had to remain on the west bank. Moevres was stormed and taken by the 57th Division on 12 September but a vigorous counter-attack on the evening of 17 September saw it back in German hands.

Inchy had been won by the 63rd (Royal Naval) Division on 3 September, it had then been held against several counter-attacks before the line advanced south and eastwards towards Moevres. The stretch of canal opposite Inchy had been only partially excavated and held no water, with banks between 2 and 3.5 metres high, but dense wire and trenches with machine gun positions on the eastern bank made it a formidable obstacle. The 44th and 46th Canadian Battalions were ordered to cross at 5.20am on 27 September. Several hours rain during the night had made the ground slippery and caused some difficulties but the Canadians overcame the limited German resistance and crossed the canal and took the trenches – the Canal du Nord Line. The 4th Bedfordshires crossed the canal in front of Moevres at the same time; they were delayed by machine guns on the east bank and were shelled with gas but took their objectives, which included the lock and Canal Trench where the Essex had fought the previous December.

To their south, in front of Demicourt, the Hindenburg Support Line was to be taken by the Guards Division on 27 September, but first they had to cross the Canal Du Nord, which was well defended. The 1st Scots Guards had little difficulty in crossing the Canal but the crossing in front of the 1st Coldstream Guards, the steel bridge carrying the

The modern bridge carrying the Demicourt- Graincourt road over the Canal. Machine guns by the far abutment prevented the Guards from crossing until silenced by the Coldstreams.

Cyril Hubert Frisby
VC

Demicourt-Graincourt road, had been blown by the Germans who positioned two machine guns beneath the fallen steelwork on the far bank (**no. 18 on map**). Lieutenant C.H. Frisby and Private T.H. Jackson slid down the west bank and, under intense point-blank machine gun fire, charged the posts and enabled the others to cross. For this both Guardsmen were awarded the VC. Frisby survived but Jackson was killed, he is buried in the nearby Sanders Keep Cemetery. This is one of the very few instances of a double VC incident, and of one of the winners lying within view of his outstanding action.

Thomas Norman
Jackson VC

THE AREA TODAY

The D15E road bridge over the Canal was replaced after the war but the difficulties the machine gun positions caused can be seen (photo above). The commanding view of the Graincourt Line over the Canal du Nord can be appreciated from the pill boxes still standing on the high ground to the east, **no. 19 on map**.

Canal Trench does not exist now but the bunker where it met the sunken road between Moevres and Graincourt can still be entered. Inside will be seen an innovative door frame used by the builders – an

105

iron bed frame.

On the edge of Quarry Wood (actually a group of small copses) is the Cemetery of that name, mainly containing the bodies of the Canadians who fought here in late September 1918. Immediately behind the cemetery, in one copse, is the large hollow from an old chalk cutting which gave the name. The hollow was a natural siting for the command centre for the Germans holding this sector and the remains of their dugouts and concrete shelters can still be traced. Nearby are the remains of several pill boxes which housed machine guns covering the land towards the canal and Moevres.

The main Hindenburg Line trenches were filled in long ago but in Tadpole Copse, just inside the northeast edge, can be found a shallow position which was right on the front line captured by the Queen's Westminster Rifles and which was later used as a defensive post by the London Scottish.

Just before Inchy is entered on the Boursies road is the pill box which defended the approach to the village, and by the D14E to the west is the command centre, now sealed from entry.

The pill boxes at Quarry Wood fired on the Ulstermen trying to capture Moevres at the start of the Battle of Cambrai, they also caused many casualties to the Canadians here in September 1918. (no. 20 on map).

1
HAVRINCOURT

The retreating Germans were pushed out of Metz on 4 April, 1917 by the 10th and 11th King's Royal Rifle Corps of the 20th (Light) Division after a good deal of fighting; resistance had been stronger than expected but by mid-afternoon the village was cleared and cellars and dugouts mopped up and a number of prisoners taken. The 11th Rifle Brigade then tried to approach and enter Havrincourt Wood but were prevented by German machine guns along the southern and southwestern edges. Several attempts were made to dislodge the defenders during which many casualties were caused; particularly troublesome was a machine gun in the southwest corner which was eventually silenced by a patrol working from the right along the edge of the wood. A week later, on 10 April (Easter Monday), the 7th Somerset Light Infantry and the 7th Duke of Cornwall's Light Infantry launched an attack: at 4pm they took the Germans – who were having their evening meal – by surprise. Casualties were very light and the British troops pushed well into the wood before enjoying the meal the Germans had prepared for themselves. Several more thrusts were necessary before the wood was fully in British hands, on 25 April the Germans were finally driven behind the Hindenburg Line defences. The British then set-to and started to organise front and rear defences in the wood; the position was found to be favourable as the high ground gave good observation to the north and the east, but just as importantly the wood gave cover to the works being carried on, which included defences, ammunition and stores dumps, troop accommodation, medical aid posts and various administrative headquarters. Several divisions held the line in turn, each one adding to the works on the woods. The 42nd (East Lancashire) Division spent from mid-May to mid-July in the wood, their history records it as being a quiet sector, where troops could exist in relative calm: 'Havrincourt Wood in the spring of 1917 remained a very beautiful spot amid the chaos of war'.[20] The Royal Engineers attached to the Division also found it to their liking: 'Havrincourt Wood made a quite useful screen, and it was possible to approach the front line in comfort and security. The weather was good, and those who lived in the wood itself found conditions quite delightful'[21].

During their tenancy, as with later divisions, works continued. More trenches and strongpoints were dug, huts erected, roads improved and several trench railway lines were laid. A number of raids were carried out by both sides, with the British continually trying to capture small patches of land and reduce No Man's Land whilst taking prisoners for intelligence purposes. On 3 July at 11pm the 7th Manchesters, under Lieutenant A. Hodge, raided the German lines and took three prisoners, killing several others with no casualties to themselves. Similar success was found by the Queen Victoria's Rifles on the night of 22 July: Second Lieutenants H.S. Prince and J.L. Worlledge, with 81 other ranks and two Royal Engineers, raided a trench mortar and machine gun position in the front line. They had their very detailed plans included changing tunic buttons in case of capture and specific objectives for each member. A number of Germans were killed and two taken prisoner for interogation, whilst all Q.V.R. members returned although one, Rifleman Lewthwaite, died from a wound through the lungs several hours after he was carried back to the lines. Luck was with the other side when, several months later the 1st Royal Irish Fusiliers held the same sector; the Germans traversed the same part of No Mans Land and took six Irishmen prisoner.

The 62nd (West Lancashire) Division used the wood to conceal artillery, tanks and troops for its attack on the Hindenburg line on 20, November 1917. The 2/7th West Yorkshires were to attack the German front line – Unseen Trench to the south east of Havrincourt. Preparations had been precise: 'a good breakfast was issued to all companies after they were formed up'[22] although the tanks which were to accompany them were 20 minutes late. C Company were detailed to attack first and take the front trench, they were successful and took 100 prisoners and four machine guns before mopping up the area.

A, B and D Companies then passed through them and took the second line objectives, reforming on the small road running east out of the village. Havrincourt and the defences in front of it were allocated to the 2/6th West Yorkshires, they were to take the village from the south and east but their tanks also did not arrive. Strong opposition was met and the front troops became engaged in heavy fighting with many losses; on reaching the first trench the troops mistakenly thought that they had captured the main Hindenburg Line but it was only the outpost trench. An Intelligence Officer, Second Lieutenant J. Moor, was sent forward from Battalion Headquarters to assess the situation, he found that casualties were 60% and the front line had not been reached. He pushed C Company forward to take Unseen Trench. Captain W.

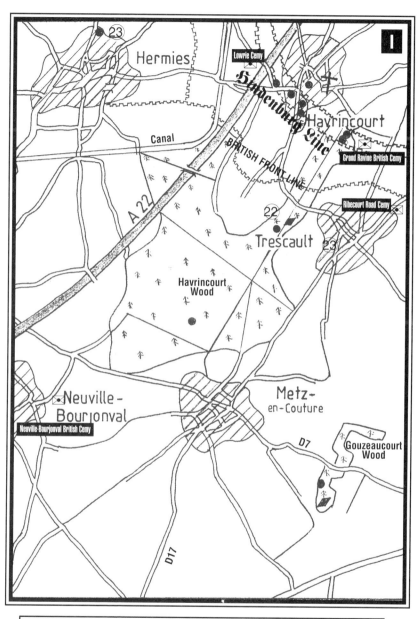

Main trench line
Site of interest
Memorial
Existing structure, British or German, e.g. pill box
Cemeteries

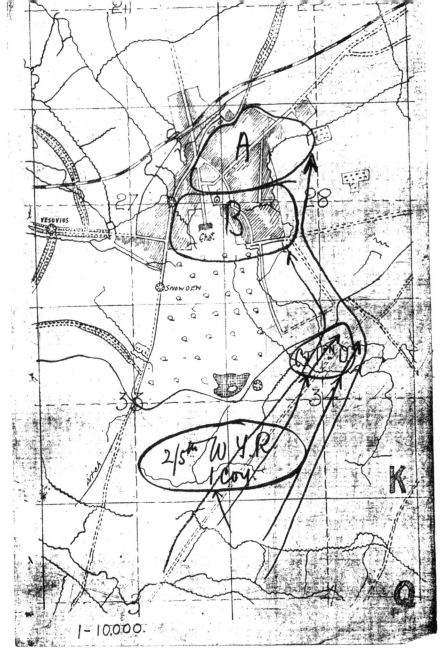

The map used by the 2/7 West Yorkshires who were to clear the Hindenburg Line, at the point where the British cemetery now stands, then Havrincourt village. The road craters marked 'Snowden' and 'Vesuvius' had been made by the Germans to prevent vehicles from using the road. The map shows how C Company then D Company attacked the trenches in the wood, then A and B Companies cleared the village, while a company of 2/5th West Yorkshires went northwards through the woods.

110

Moorhouse then led A Company through the Hindenburg Line and together with B Company they took the village; by 10.15am the Hindenburg Line and the eastern side of the village had been cleared. Meanwhile the 2/4th and 2/5th King's Own Yorkshire Light Infantry were clearing the Hindenburg Line on the western edge of the village, the trenches were won only after hand-to-hand fighting, during which 400 Germans were taken prisoner.

Havrincourt Chateau had been a particularly well defended strongpoint from where machine guns had rained fire on the attackers before being silenced; seventy Germans were taken prisoner in the chateau and the dugouts beneath. The battle then moved away towards Bourlon in the northeast.

In March 1918 the 17th (Northern) Division held the villages of Hermies and Havrincourt, now the rear of the Flesquières Salient, when the German assault began. The 7th Lincolnshires were in Hermies, with the 12th Manchesters in Havrincourt. The early German attacks were beaten off but eventually succeeded.

This section of the Hindenburg Line was to be the scene of severe fighting again when, during their retreat in September 1918, the Germans decided to make another stand here. The British 42nd (East Lancashire) Division were in Havrincourt Wood preparing for another assault on the front line when, on the night of 21 September the

This brick and steel dug-out on the edge of Hermies was used as a command post by the 7th Lincolnshires who defended the village in March 1918. It was probably built by the Royal Engineers of the 36th (Ulster) Division when they set out the defences as the Germans fell back onto the Hindenburg Line (no. 23 on map).

Germans sent almost 3000 Yellow Cross (BB-dichlor-ethyl-sulphide, or mustard gas) shells into the wood, causing severe casualties.

The Lancastrians and Mancunians continued with their arrangements for the assault and, with the 3rd Division on their left, on the morning of 27 September, after a short but intense artillery barrage, they stormed and overran Unseen Trench and the support lines behind. Losses on both sides were high.

The machine gun post in the grounds of Havrincourt Chateau.

THE AREA TODAY

Havrincourt Wood today is a peaceful place, with little traffic noise or modern sounds to break the silence. The rides through the trees are the same layout as during the war, and some of the ground is uneven, otherwise there is little to show that the wood was once home to several thousand men with numerous dugouts (most of which were stripped for building material in the 1920's), gun emplacements, railways and stores areas. A concrete dugout [**marked 22 on map**] dug and concreted by 150 Field Company, Royal Engineers for the 62nd Division whilst they tenanted the wood, has concrete stairs leading down into it and a brickwork retaining wall. Of the numerous other dugouts not many remain: two can be identified by the brick and steel remains in the wood. On the edge of the Wood facing Trescault was a small lime quarry which contained a Brigade Headquarters in dugouts dug into the quarry walls, these have now collapsed but can be identified by the collapses. The British front line trenches, Trescault Trench and Support, can be identified as can a front line machine gun position on the eastern edge. Close to the British cemetery outside Havrincourt village, just inside the trees, can be found the (now shallow) Unseen Trench, the front line of the Hindenburg system. This includes two concrete dugouts, the remaining ones of those cleared by C Company of the 2/6th West Yorkshires.

On the west side of Havrincourt village there are still several front line concrete bunkers taken by the K.O.Y.L.I.s together with a steel and concrete observation post just inside the trees. This observation post was the subject of a report by the Royal Engineers.

A few metres away from this observation post is a shelter, the ice store for the Chateau which was reinforced by the Germans. Directly in front of the Chateau, in the private garden where entry is not allowed, facing down to the Ravine, is a large, circular, machine gun pill box.

The German observation post on the edge of Havrincourt Wood, several metres away from the D15. This stood right on the front of the Hindenburg Line and the occupant was able to watch the British front posts. The central core of the post is of prefabricated rolled steel, with an overlay of concrete.

The brick lined entrance to the dugout constructed by the Royal Engineers of the 62nd Division (no. 22 on map).

J
BOURLON AND FLESQUIÈRES

Graincourt village was wrested from the Germans on 20 November 1917, the opening day of the Battle of Cambrai. Having fought their way past Havrincourt and mopped up German dugouts, the 2/4th and 2/6th Duke of Wellington's of the 62nd Division, pushed into the village with the aid of three tanks which silenced some field guns at the edge of the village. the troops then pressed on to Anneux with cavalry (King Edward's Horse) but came under machine gun fire at the thick barbed wire defences and, as dark was approaching, fell back to Graincourt. They tried again the following morning and overwhelmed the garrison of the 52nd Reserve Regiment before moving through and crossing the Bapaume-Cambrai road towards Bourlon Wood, but were prevented from entering the wood by heavy fire from within and the small quarry on the edge. They held the ground between the main road and the edge of the wood through the day until being relieved by the 2/7th West Yorkshires at dusk. At dawn this battalion sent forward a platoon under Second Lieutenant Moore with a machine gun to establish a forward post at the quarry where the track enters the wood: they encountered a large party of Germans coming from the wood and dispersed them, killing most. The field of fire from this position was not good however so the platoon moved to where the wood meets the side road, the D15, into Bourlon village. Here they came under fire from machine guns in pill boxes on the edge of the wood and could not proceed further. The by now tired and exhausted Yorkshiremen were withdrawn and relieved by the 40th Division who were to be given the task of taking Bourlon village and the Wood.

Noyelles, having been entered by a cavalry patrol earlier in the day in a probe of the defences, was taken from the Germans by the 2nd Royal Fusiliers, who found many artillery shelters and concrete dugouts which were then used by the British.

The Scotsmen of the 51st (Highland) Division had not been able to enter Flesquières due partly to determined opposition from the 387th Landwehr and 27th Reserve Infantry Regiments within but also to lack

Until the summer of 1995, when most were demolished, 26 of these bunkers built into the road embankment in Noyelles existed. These were used for ammunition storage and for billeting troops, and were taken and used by the 2nd Royal Fusiliers during the Battle of Cambrai. They fell into British hands again the following year, when the 2nd South Staffords captured 300 Germans, some of whom were still clad in pyjamas.

of co-operation between tanks and infantry. Trenches – the Hindenburg Support Line – in front of the village had been entered but not held and the troops had to fall back. At 2.45am on the following morning, 21 November, A, B and D Companies of 1/7th Gordon Highlanders sent

The map used by Lieutenant Ferguson of the Gordon Highlanders when he entered Flesquières.

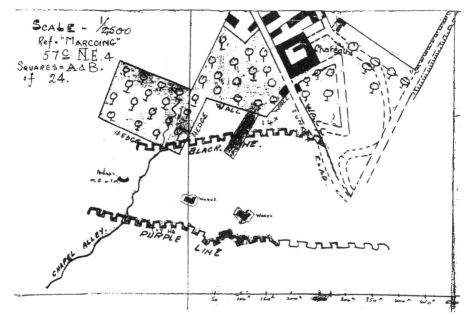

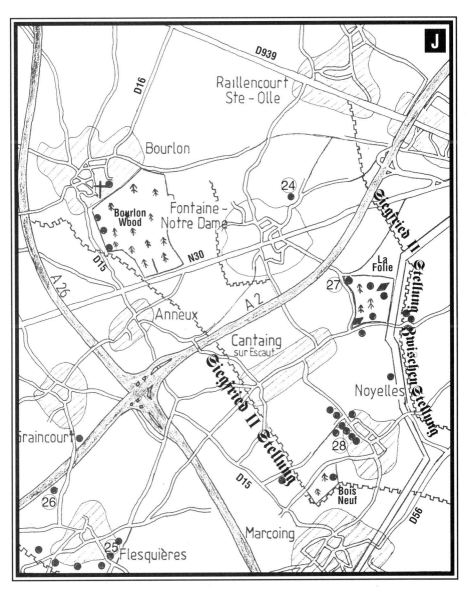

J

D939

Raillencourt
Ste - Olle

D16

Bourlon

✝

Bourlon
Wood

Fontaine -
Notre Dame

N30

D15

A 26

Anneux

A 2

Cantaing
sur Escaut

24

La
Folie

27

Siegfried II Stellung

Noyelles

Siegfried II Stellung

Zwischen Stellung

28

Graincourt

D15

Bois
Neuf

26

D56

Marcoing

25 Flesquières

⌐⌐⌐⌐⌐ Main trench line	● Existing structure, British or German, e.g. pill box
◣ Site of interest	
✝ Memorial	⊠ Cemeteries

117

patrols onto the village: A Company, under Lieutenant J.J. Ferguson, passed the trenches which had been fought over the previous day and found the village abandoned except for a few snipers; C Company then worked up the main street and entered the Chateau. The Division was also successful later in the day, Cantaing was attacked but stoutly defended by the Germans, as the 1/4th Seaforth Highlanders and 1/4th Gordon Highlanders pressed from the the west the 14th Durham Light Infantry, with tanks and cavalry, fought their way in from the southeast. The fight for the village was fierce and lasted two hours. The 1/4th Seaforth Highlanders also took the Cantaing Line north of the village and a mill, which stood close to where the Motorway now is, before moving on to Fontaine-Notre-Dame. This village had just been cleared of Germans by three tanks of H Battalion, Havoc, Hadrian and Hong so the Scotsmen worked to the end of the village but were then held up by defences which included a pill box to the north east of the village. This pill box (**marked no. 24 on map**) swept the village with its field of fire; the British front line was established at the last houses along the main road. At this furthest point of advance the commanding officer, Captain Peverell, was mortally wounded. The Seaforths were to hold the village and its perimeter with a greatly diminished force due to heavy casualties during the day but at dawn on the following day, 22 November, an overwhelming force of Germans attacked and forced the British back. On the following day tanks of B, I and C Battalions – a total of 36 machines – tried to open the village for the infantry. The tanks were not successful in built-up areas and many were put out of action in the village, some were set on fire or damaged by shells and mortars and some were disabled by German infantrymen swarming over them.

The British were determined to occupy Fontaine and ordered the Guards Division to do so on 27 November. The Guards considered the proposed plan to be ill-conceived, a dangerous and impracticable undertaking but their commanding officer, Major-General Feilding, had his objections over-ruled and the attack began at 6.20am, as snow turned to rain. The 3rd Grenadier Guards were to enter along the main Bapaume-Cambrai road whilst the 1st Coldstream were to take the area between the village and Bourlon Wood. The 1st Scots Guards were to cover the southern approaches to the village because German machine guns and artillery in La Folie Wood, to the south, were able to fire on the attackers. These guns took a heavy toll as soon as the attack began, and the Grenadiers suffered badly, some companies lost all their officers. Working through the houses was difficult, Germans were hidden in the ruins and cellars and were able to attack the Guards from

The bunker built into the gatehouse at La Folie was used by machine gunners who fired on the Guards attacking Fontaine-Notre-Dame, over the valley. The gatehouse was later rebuilt, and used by the Germans again in the 1940's and carved graffiti can be found in the soft stonework. The wood of La Folie still contains a number of other Hindenburg Line relics but is private property.

the rear but the Guards fought on and at 7.15am reached their first objective, the church in the centre. The attack continued; the Grenadiers pushed further through the village, their progress impeded by parties of Germans who were using two derelict tanks as strongpoints. A greatly depleted force reached the eastern end of the village but were too few to advance further and were now under intense fire from German machine guns to the northeast. The Coldstream had also lost many officers and men working through the north of the houses; the remnants captured the railway station with fifty prisoners and two field guns but could not move further forward and were then shelled out of this position, destroying the two German guns before they fell back. A German counter-attack was repulsed but the Coldstream and the Grenadiers on their right, together with the Irish Guards who had been attacking through the eastern edge of Bourlon wood, were ordered to fall back to their starting lines. The battle was over by 2pm, and had cost the Guards 38 officers and 1,043 men, of whom nine officers and 481 men were missing.

La Folie Wood was a strong position which guarded the approach to Bourlon and contained a main stores depot fed by a rail link and a barge dock on the Escaut Canal. On its southern edge were positions which

The pill box on the outskirts of Fontaine-Notre-Dame (known by the Germans as an *Igel* or hedgehog on account of it's bristling field of fire) which stopped the advance of the Guards (no. 24 on map).

guarded the approaches to the Canal; British cavalry (4th Dragoon Guards) reached this and entered the wood before leaving when German infantry arrived.

Bourlon Wood and village, which the 62nd Division had been unable to take on 20 November, was the objective of the 40th Division on 23rd. The wood was thickly timbered and sat on top of a ridge, rising to forty

One of the pill boxes on the edge of Bourlon Wood. The South Wales Borderers took them from the Prussian Guards and on 30 November 1917 the 15th Londons used them to beat off a German attack from the north west. These survived the planned demolition by 520 Field Company Royal Engineers during the British withdrawal from the Wood.

metres above the Bapaume-Cambrai road, giving distant views to the east, which was why both sides wanted it.

At 10.30am the 12th South Wales Borderers and 19th Royal Welch Fusiliers, aided by tanks, fought their way through the Wood, coming under heavy machine gun fire as they did so. The South Wales Borderers entered the Wood at the southwest corner and worked their way up the western edge, encountering some German pill boxes manned by the Prussian Guards. Infantry and tanks – who had not worked together before – helped each other and eventually the pill boxes and other strong points were overcome and by noon a company of South Wales Borderers had reached the outskirts of Bourlon village, meanwhile the centre and eastern half of the Wood had been taken by the Royal Welch Fusiliers. The high ground to the west of the wood was also now in British hands and the 20th Middlesex, which had suffered many losses from the pill boxes on the western edge of the Wood, were able to send patrols into Bourlon village at 2pm. It was apparent that the village could not be captured and the gains made were consolidated in expectation of a German counter-attack. The British attack was resumed the following day; the 14th Highland Light Infantry and 12th Suffolks forced the German defenders out of their positions and passed through the village but not all positions were overcome and both sides became entangled, not knowing where the others were. The village was effectively a No Mans Land: the Germans again resumed control and further fortified the village by hiding field artillery and machine guns in houses and constructing strong barricades. Two days later the 2/5th West Yorkshires and 2/5th King's Own Yorkshire Light Infantry followed 15 tanks into the village. After two hours the remains of the infantry and five tanks withdrew and the British planners realised that the village was impregnable, and no more plans were hatched.

With the British front line running between the wood and the village, the 47th (London) Division took over the positions in the Wood. On their first night in the wood, 28/29 November,the wood was heavily bombarded with 16,000 gas shells and many troops were gassed. On 30 November, as part of a major attempt to push the British back, the Germans tried to push the Londoners off the high ground in the wood but were unable to do so, one of their main obstacles for the attack from the northwest was the Londoners machine guns in the former German pill boxes on the edge of the wood.

The decision was taken to withdraw immediately from the wood and, on the night of 4 December the 47th Division retired from it in accordance with instructions. 520 Field Company, Royal Engineers of the division were instructed to destroy all defences, dugouts and

The light signaling station, or *blinkstelle*, which the Germans built behind Flesquières Chateau to communicate with Cambrai was later used as an observation post by the British. The underground chamber is sealed off and the regimental emblem over the door has been removed but its laurel leaf surround still remains.

captured German artillery but little time was allowed.

The land passed back to the Germans included Cantaing, Anneux and Graincourt, the British front line was established just in front of Flesquières.

Bourlon Wood and village were to be defended again by the Germans: on 27 September 1918 the 11th and 12th Canadian Brigades went forward towards remnants of the trees and houses. German

This pill box, next to the Graincourt-Flesquières road where it crosses the motorway, was built inside a hunting lodge which stood here. It has embrasures for all-round fire from the two machine guns within. For two days, at the start of the Battle of Cambrai, it was the German front line as it helped to hold up the advance of the 62nd Division making for Bourlon Wood. It was later a British front line post when the Flesquières Salient was formed.

defence was stiff but soon overcome and for deeds on the western edge of the wood two Canadian officers were awarded the VC, Lieutenants S.L. Honey and G.T. Lyall. On the next day, 28 September, the 43rd Canadian Battalion secured Fontaine-Notre-Dame.

The Hindenburg Support Line (the Graincourt Line) on the slight rise to the west of Graincourt contained several pill boxes which put up a strong defence and held up the Guards and 2nd Divisions which crossed the Canal du Nord on 27 September, 1918. These pill boxes and Graincourt village were attacked from the northwest by the 57th Division, the 2nd Grenadier Guards were then able to continue and take Orival Wood after tackling and taking two pill boxes which caused casualties on the way.

Samuel Lewis Honey VC

Graham Thomson Lyall VC

Nine Wood (Bois Neuf) and the many dugouts and bunkers it contained was captured by the 1st King's Royal Rifle Corps, the Germans retiring with little resistance. Only one, on the eastern edge, of the many bunkers still remains. The K.R.R.C's then proceded to capture Noyelles with the 2nd South Staffords; in the village they took prisoner 300 Germans in the many concrete shelters there, some of whom were still clad in pyjamas. The village contained a battery of 77mm field guns and several heavy howitzers, and many machine guns and trench mortars which were prized booty. However the troops were unable to procede across the canal because of machine gun fire from the far side and the west bank was the limit of the days advance.

THE AREA TODAY

Around Flesquières and Graincourt can be found much of the Hindenburg Support Line (Graincourt Line) which caused so many problems and hold-ups in November 1917 and then again in September 1918. On the southern edge of Flesquières are several pill boxes which held up the 51st (Highland) Division on 20 November but were taken on the following day by Lieutenant J.J. Ferguson and A Company, 7th Gordon Highlanders, on their way into the village. Close by, on the other side of the brick wall bordering the road [**no. 25 on map**] is a steel circular observation post of the same pattern as the one on the edge of Havrincourt Wood. The rear wall of the Chateau grounds has a large light signalling station (*blinkstelle*) which sent signals back to Cambrai.

Close to the motorway are two pill boxes [**no. 26 on map**] which were

123

used by the Germans to great effect, the one on the northern side was built inside a hunters lodge which stood here. West of Graincourt, on the slightly higher ground, can be seen several pill boxes and bunkers of the main defence line.

In Bourlon village, off the D16 from Sains-le-Marquion, the remains of the old brick perimeter walls of the Chateau still stand 4 metres high and show the scars of shell and bullet from the fighting in 1917 and 1918. Bourlon Wood still contains many scars from the repeated battles for it's possession; many shallow trench lines and broken ground can be found. On the western edge of the wood are the three concrete pill boxes which prevented the advance of the British on the first day of the Battle of Cambrai, and were later used to prevent a German counter attack. The southern entrance to the wood and quarry was the forward post established by Second Lieutenant Moore and 2/7th West Yorkshires. To the northeast of Fontaine-Notre-Dame is the concrete machine gun emplacement which prevented the British from pressing further than this village on several occasions.

Facing Fontaine across the valley, now containing the motorway, is La Folie Wood. The entrance to the wood – which is private property – is guarded by an ornate gate house, rebuilt in the 1920's but still attached is a concrete bunker [**no. 27 on map**] which shows how it was built into the original structure. From here German machine gunners fired upon the Guards attacking Fontaine, killing many Scots and

The concrete emplacement for a heavy gun near Nine Wood (Bois Neuf). One of the few constructions in the area to be built with pre-cast concrete blocks.

Grenadier Guardsmen. The gate house was used again by a later occupying force; in the soft limestone of the facing is carved graffiti: J. Smidth 1.6.41., H.B. Poessnek 30.4.41, Herbert Schirmacher and Ernst Eeyxa were both there there 17.11.43 and several swastikas are clear. Of the many railway sidings in the wood none now exist but there can be found the steel posts of the military station and concrete platform, also several concrete shelters. On the southern edge of the wood, by the D92, is the one remaining wall of a house ruined by shell fire.

Noyelles-sur-Escaut contained a line of 26 concrete shelters until the summer of 1995, when most were demolished although several were retained as examples [**no. 28 on map**] and several ruined shelters can be found 150 metres further along the street and a small bunker is opposite the side of the village cemetery. On the eastern edge of Nine Wood (Bois Neuf) is a concrete bunker which was a command post for German artillery batteries in the wood. The wood contained a small quarry which was an important command centre with many dugouts but in recent years the quarry was filled with waste. Close by is a gun emplacement, with concrete casing, which housed a heavy gun.

One of the cluster of German bunkers on what was 'Kaiser Trench', marked no.30 on map. After being captured by the 2nd Sherwood Foresters it was used by the 47th and 63rd Divisions before being yielded back to the Germans.

K

GOUZEAUCOURT AND RIBÉCOURT

The battle moved into this area in April 1917 when the Germans were being pushed back to their prepared positions in the Hindenburg Line. The area had been devastated but the defenders did not want to give it up without a struggle.

The first operations were in the early afternoon of 4 April when the 10th and 11th Rifle Brigades of the 20th (Light) Division advanced towards Gouzeaucourt Wood and came under heavy machine gun fire from within the wood, suffering many casualties. Also attacking the wood were the 2nd Rifle Brigade and the 2nd Royal Berkshires of the 8th Division. Snow was falling and visibility hampered both attackers and defenders and the attack developed into a series of scattered and isolated fights. During one of these skirmishes Captain the Hon. A.M. Bertie of the 11th Rifle Brigade tried to silence the the machine guns and was awarded the D.S.O. for his bravery. Eventually all objectives were taken, although it was to be another week before the line moved forward again.

Heavy snow was again falling on the evening of 12 April when the 2nd East Lancashires and the 1st Sherwood Foresters attacked the German defenders in Gouzeaucourt village. The attack was a surprise and a success and by 9.45pm the village was in British hands and its defenders either dead or taken prisoner. There was then one village, Gonnelieu, between the British and the main German defences where it was presumed the advance would be held up. The capture of this village was important as it overlooked the British positions; during 19 and 20 April the village defences were shelled and attempts made to cut the masses of barbed wire for an attack on 21 April. At 4.20am on that day the 2nd Lincolnshires, preceded by a heavy artillery barrage, managed to get through the wire and enter the village. After heavy fighting the village was captured and its defenders taken prisoner. At the same time the 40th Division won the high ground to the northwest; these ridges were stubbornly defended by the Germans, especially where ravines cut into them and made good defensive positions.

The ridge immediately north of Gonnelieu was taken by the 19th

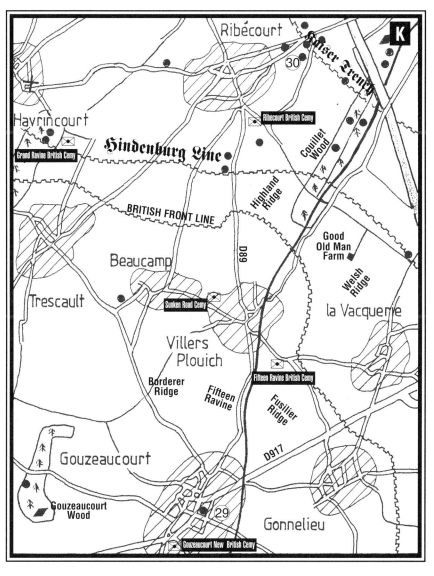

K

Ribécourt

Ulster Trench

30

Havrincourt

Ribécourt British Cemy

Grand Ravine British Cemy

Hindenburg Line

Couillet Wood

BRITISH FRONT LINE

Highland Ridge

D89

Good Old Man Farm

Welsh Ridge

Beaucamp

Trescault

Sunken Road Cemy

la Vacquerie

Villers Plouich

Borderer Ridge

Fifteen Ravine

Fifteen Ravine British Cemy

Fusilier Ridge

D917

Gouzeaucourt

Gouzeaucourt Wood

29

Gonnelieu

Gouzeaucourt New British Cemy

ⴖⴖⴖⴖⴖⴖⴖ Main trench line
◣ Site of interest
╋ Memorial

● Existing structure, British or German, e.g. pill box
⊠ Cemeteries

Royal Welsh Fusiliers, and was then given the name Fusilier Ridge. Another ridge to the west of this was attacked by the 12th South Wales Borderers; the Germans clung on tenaciously and machine gun and snipers posts checked the advance. Fighting around Fifteen Ravine (named after 15 trees which stood there until felled during German devastations) was particularly severe. The ravine contained a number of machine gun positions, snipers posts and deep mined dugouts and was defended by 150 Germans. Eventually the Borderers wrested control of the ravine and the ridge, which was subsequently named Borderer Ridge.

The main villages which were now still in German hands but in front of the Hindenburg Line were Villers Plouich, Beaucamp and la Vaquerie. The 13th East Surrey Regiment was given the task of capturing Villers Plouich and at 4.15pm on 24 April the battalion, lead

Edward FosterVC

by Captain L.B. Mills, left their trenches and went forward. At 5.30pm they reached the village and came under heavy machine gun fire from within. Two German machine guns caused many casualties but these were captured and the crews taken prisoner by Corporal Foster, who was awarded the VC and Lance-Corporal Reed, who received the DCM for their actions. Five other members of the battalion won the MM during the fighting in the village. As soon as the village was lost to the Germans they began to shell heavily the ruins in which the East Surreys tried to find shelter. Meanwhile the 14th Argyll and Sutherland Highlanders were trying to capture Beaucamp but were having difficulties. They had been held up by uncut wire and hidden machine guns around the hamlet. Beaucamp was entered by troops but they were forced to retire after heavy casualties. Another attempt was then made to gain a foothold but the attackers were driven off by the Germans within. British artillery bombarded the defenders and the following day the 11th King's Own Regiment entered and consolidated the ruins without difficulty. This was made possible by the capture of the high ground to the east of Trescault by the 20th Division, from where the Germans had had good observation over Beaucamp.

All of the land in front of the Hindenburg Line in this sector was now under British tenancy, except for la Vaquerie. It was expected that this would be vigorously defended. British plans were drawn up to capture the village and incorporate it into the British defences but these were then changed and the intended capture was replaced by a large raid by the 8th and 40th Divisions; the raid was to take place during the dark. At 11pm on 5 May it began but problems occurred in many areas. The village was entered by 12th South Wales Borderers but other battalions were held up by uncut wire, lost direction in the dark or encountered obstinate defenders. The troops withdrew before first light; the raid was not considered a great success although lessons had been learnt. The Germans then decided permanently to keep the village and it was included in their defence zone as a forward line of the *Siegfriedstellung*.

The area then became relatively quiet for the rest of the summer. The Germans continued to bolster their defences on one side whilst the British began the task of organising theirs, whilst constructing camps for troops, repairing roads and railways and settling into the land which had been devastated by the Germans and had been fought over.

NOVEMBER 1917

The main line railway running northwards out of Villers Plouich was the dividing line between the two divisions which attacked on this front. To the right the 20th (Light) Division had the objectives of capturing la Vaquerie, which had had substantial improvements to its defences and was now part of the Hindenburg Line proper, and the high ground of Welsh Ridge. The general direction of the attack was northeast, secrecy for the preparations had been assisted by mist which had not cleared for several days. At zero hour – 6.20am on 20 November – the artillery barrage which preceded the infantry attack opened up along the whole front. Tanks of I Battalion rolled forward to the village, with infantry following behind. The defending Germans were evidently surprised and scared by the tanks and retired, leaving their positions to the 7th Somerset Light Infantry, which entered at 7.30am and had mopped up by 9am. Other tank and infantry units swept up Welsh Ridge, overcoming defences and swarming over German trenches, although artillery bombardments began to thin numbers and destroy tanks.

Albert Edward Shepherd VC

As the ridge was traversed the opposition stiffened and began to slow the advance. Progress was maintained however: the 12th King's Royal Rifle Corps were held up by a machine gun position on the ridge until Rifleman A.E. Shepherd rushed forward and killed the gunners, an act for which he was rewarded with the VC. Also awarded the VC (posthumously) for bravery on the ridge was Captain R.W.L. Wain, whose tank was hit by a shell during the attack on Good Old Man Farm, which was only 100 metres in front of the main Hindenburg Line front trench and was strongly defended. Taking the Lewis gun from the wreckage he rushed the stronghold in the farm and drove the Germans out, firing at them as they fell back. He was then killed by a bullet in the head but the infantry were able to proceed to

Richard William Leslie Wain VC

their next objective, the main trench line. To the left of the railway the 6th Division was taking its objectives on schedule and were little hampered by German artillery, which was weak and ineffective. The 1st Buffs worked its way through and along Couillet Wood, clearing it of Germans. Ribécourt was entered by infantry before the tanks had reached the village, although they were needed when some troublesome machine guns were encountered. The 9th Norfolk Regiment, together with the 2nd Sherwood Foresters, had taken almost 200 prisoners by the time they considered the village clear. Another trench system – Kaiser Trench and Support – was then attacked with the assistance of the tanks. An important command centre was over-run, the 2nd Sherwood Foresters took prisoner a Regimental Commander and three other officers and made their tally for the day 290 prisoners. The command centre included several large concrete dugouts, these were used as headquarters by a number of British units over the coming winter.

Following a withdrawal of the front line by the 47th (London) Division on the night of 14 January 1918 these dugouts were now on the British front line and were adapted for defence by the Royal Engineers. They were used by the 63rd (Royal Naval) Division when the Germans made their major offensive on 21 and 22 March.

The advances made during the Battle of Cambrai were under pressure from counter-attack and on the morning of 30 November the 12th (Eastern) and 20th (Light) Divisions were pushed out of Gouzeaucourt after attempts by a Field Company of Royal Engineers, together with some assorted transport men and American engineers who had been constructing a light railway in the village, to hold the attackers back. A determined attack to retake the village was carried out at short notice by the Coldstream Guards with the 20th Hussars. Sweeping down from Gouzeaucourt Wood, on foot and under machine gun fire, they fought their way into the village. Coming under fire from British artillery pieces which had earlier been abandoned and were now being used by the Germans, they took control of the village, most of the

Germans retreated or were killed. By 1pm the fighting was over, the Guards had taken about a hundred prisoners and the gun batteries, complete with ammunition and stores, were handed back to the artillery.

At 6.20am on the following day the Guards tried to recapture Gonnelieu but found the village to be full of Germans who were massing for an attack of their own. The 4th Grenadiers managed to get as far as the eastern edge of the village but were forced out by the German defenders. Losses were high and the survivors were in danger of being overwhelmed; Captain George

George Henry
Totham Paton
VC

130

This German command bunker, together with a number of German officers, was captured by the 2nd Sherwood Foresters at the start of the Battle of Cambrai. It was then used as headquarters by several British battalions, until the night of 14 January 1918 when the 47th (London) Division who held this sector withdrew from the high ground to the northwest. This bunker then became a front line post, being prepared for defence by 520 Field Company, Royal Engineers. The bunker was manned by Hawke Battalion of the 63rd (Royal Naval) Division when the Germans attacked at 5.45am on 21 March 1918, having deluged the area in mustard gas. Fighting was intense throughout the day; at 3pm Drake Battalion gave support and more attacks were beaten off. At 7.48pm that evening the order was received to evacuate this front line position and it was given up to the Germans. During the summer of 1993 the bunker was excavated and opened up; around the doorway and in front were many used Lewis gun panniers and much small arms ammunition from the stand made by Hawke and Drake Battalions.

Henry Totham Paton rallied his troops on the western edge under fire and held the line before being killed. He was posthumously awarded the VC.

The Germans retained control of Gonnelieu for the rest of the winter and the village became an outpost zone of the Hindenburg Line.

THE SPRING 1918 OFFENSIVE

Battalions of the 9th (Scottish) Division were holding Gouzeaucourt when the German attack began on 21 March 1918. The village was the northernmost of the 5th Army, and its defences were expected to act as a flank if required. During the course of the morning the Highlanders in the village sat out a prolonged bombardment of gas and high explosive shells; at 10am the German infantry made a determined effort to wrest control of the village but the Scots held firm and beat the attackers back. Fighting was then continuous throughout the day but the attackers did not manage to gain any ground. During the evening the division was ordered to withdraw from the village.

The 47th (London) Division held the front between la Vaquerie and Villers Plouich. On the morning of 21 March the front and reserve trenches received a continuous rain of explosive and gas shells. Rear areas – headquarters, camps, depots and crossroads – were also bombarded and communications were made very difficult. During the evening the division, together with the 63rd (Royal Naval) Division on its left, left the front line and withdrew to a line west of Villers Plouich

This British pill box, constructed by the Royal Engineers (probably 64 Field Company) for the 9th (Scottish) Division, was manned by A Company, 9th Battalion Machine Gun Corps when the 120th and 123rd (Württemburg) Infantry Regiments attacked at 10am on 21 March 1918. The Württemburgers reached the valley in front of the pill box and got close before machine gun fire reduced their numbers and forced them to retreat. The pill box was abandoned later in the evening.

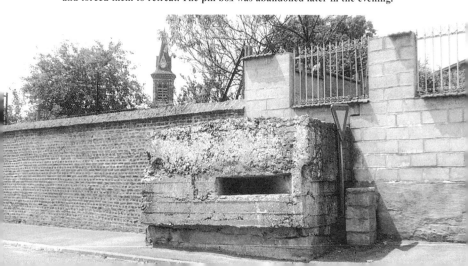

and Couillet Wood. The Germans stormed this position three times but were beaten back by the 18th London Regiment (London Irish). A fourth attempt was then made but the London Irish again stopped them, then counter attacked, cut off and annihilated the attackers.

To the north the Germans had attacked the British in front of Ribémont: Drake and Hood Naval Battalions had taken over this sector a month earlier and the front line trenches had originally been Kaiser Trench, part of the Hindenburg support line. The gas and high explosive bombardment started at 4.45am and lasted until 5.45am when the Germans appeared out of the morning mist and succeeded in entering the trenches and forcing the defenders back. Fighting then moved further westwards and the area again became a quiet German rear zone for the rest of the summer.

By late September, 1918 the Germans were again falling back to the Hindenburg Line and were preparing for another defensive battle. The 42nd (East Lancashire) Division were pressing them backwards but were suffering heavy casualties from determined rear guard actions. On the morning of 27 September the 7th and 8th Lancashire Fusiliers leading companies were virtually wiped out by machine gun fire from within Beaucamp; the 5th Manchesters also suffered heavy losses during their advance on the Hindenburg Line, this section of which was named Unseen Trench. The 7th Manchesters emptied dugouts of Germans in Unseen Trench and Unseen Support, batches of 20 and 30 prisoners were taken in the large and elaborate shelters. The Hindenburg Line had again been pierced and the Lancastrians pushed onwards. The 10th Manchesters and the 5th Lancashire Fusiliers won the high ground of Highland Ridge which the London Irish had defended earlier in the year, the 10th Manchesters then cleared Couillet Wood of Germans and crossed the railway. On their left the 1st Auckland Infantry Battalion overran the defences of the Hindenburg Support – Kaiser Trench – and retook the concrete bunkers which had already changed hands several times.

THE AREA TODAY

A number of interesting remains and relics of the 1917 and 1918 fighting can be found in the region. In Gouzeaucourt village is the British pill box used on the first day of the German spring offensive, marked 29 on the map. Several bunkers are in Couillet Wood but these are on private land and access is very limited. The foresters house contains cellars which were strengthened with thick reinforced concrete as a shell

Unseen Trench, the German front line trench won by the Mancunians and Lancastrians of the 42nd Division, and the entrance to a dug-out, shortly after its capture.

proof shelter by the Germans, the existing house was rebuilt over the cellars in later years. In the wood was a stores and ammunition dump fed by a spur off the main railway. Two large concrete bunkers, each with several rooms, which were part of the dump, are still in the wood, the track of the light railway is just discernible. The German command bunkers which were later used by the British are by the Ribécourt-Marcoing road [**marked 30 on the map**]. Also near here is a spring which was dammed by the Germans in 1917 to ensure a water supply. The stone wall forming a large sink or trough for horses still bears the inscription of the Jäger Regiment:

J.R. 31 1917

The spring was used again by a later occupying army which also left an inscription, together with a carved swastika:

S.K.P. 2/84 1940

The spring, which is still used as a source of mineral water by the locals, is in the trees down the small road signposted 'source' off the Marcoing-Ribécourt road. Nearby are two German concrete dugouts built into the rail embankment.

Rolled steel observation post, minus roof, just inside the perimeter wall of the chateau captured by the 7th Gordon Highlanders. This is the end of the 'Black Line' on the map on page 116. An identical pattern observation post can be found on the edge of Havrincourt Wood.

L

EPEHY AND VILLERS GUISLAIN

Epehy, with the adjoining village of Peizières, stands on top of a ridge which was eagerly sought by both sides. The Germans, on siting the Hindenburg Line, saw it as a valuable outpost position which gave good artillery observation over the approaching British and were determined to hold on to it. To the British it was an important strategic site which must be taken if they were to succeed in hemming in the Germans - the value of its high position and field of view was seen well before the village itself was seen. To the east the land falls away into several valleys, sloping down to the Canal de St. Quentin, 6 kilometres away. The front line of the main Hindenberg Line crossed the canal just south of Vendhuile, rising on either side to Bony and La Terrière, and Epehy allowed good observation over this stretch – observation which the Germans wanted to deny to their enemies.

The capture of the village from the rear guard of the retiring Germans began on 30 March 1917 when they lost the hamlet of St. Emilie to the 1/4th Gloucestershires of the 48th Division. This toe-hold on the ridge allowed the attackers to form up for an assault the following day. Three battalions of the 48th Division – the 7th Worcestershires, the 6th Gloucestershires and the 6th Royal Warwickshires – carried out an attack which came as a surprise to the defenders as no artillery was used. The village and 26 of its former garrison were then in British hands, although the Germans had not yet been pushed right back and were only just outside the village.

Heavy snow fell over the next few days and made further fighting difficult, the front was static and defences were dug and wired on the eastern edge. The division pressed it's attack again on 5 April – the dual villages of Lempire and Ronssoy were attacked without prior artillery bombardment. Thick belts of barbed wire held up the infantry, after these were overcome the villages were taken house by house. British losses were high – 141 killed or wounded – but the new occupants were at least pleased to find a supply of new underclothes in a captured store.

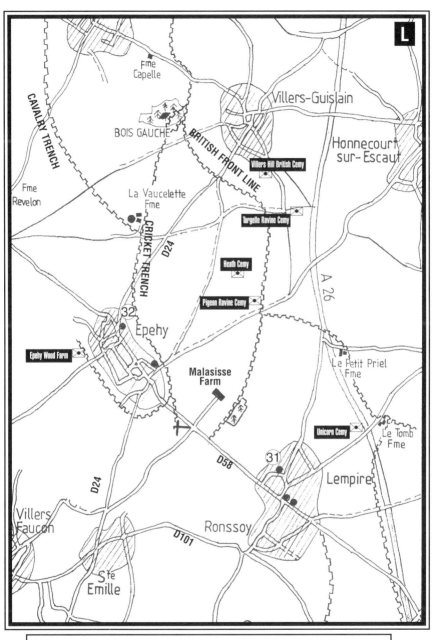

Fme
Capelle

BOIS GAUCHE

Villers-Guislain

CAVALRY TRENCH

BRITISH FRONT LINE

Villers Hill British Cemy

Honnecourt
sur-Escaut

Fme
Revelon

La Vaucelette
Fme

CRICKET TRENCH

D24

Targelle Ravine Cemy

Heath Cemy

A 26

Pigeon Ravine Cemy

32

Epehy

Epehy Wood Farm

Malasisse
Farm

Le Petit Priel
Fme

Unicorn Cemy

Le Tomb
Fme

D58

31

Lempire

Villers
Faucon

D24

Ronssoy

Ste
Emille

D101

⊔⊓⊔⊓⊔⊓ Main trench line	● Existing structure, British or German, e.g. pill box
◢ Site of interest	
✝ Memorial	⊠ Cemeteries

The 42nd Division, recently arrived from Egypt where they had been defending the Suez Canal, and still partly equipped for that climate, took over the village on 8 April. Unused to the weather, which was still very wintry, the Manchester and Lancashire Fusilier battalions huddled in the front line trenches and shell holes for their first experiences on the Western Front. They had a number of skirmishes with the Germans as the line was still being slowly advanced. They held Malassise Farm as a position; during a relief of the 7th Lancashire Fusiliers by the 6th the farm was heavily shelled. The building was destroyed and 50 men were buried in the cellar. Rescue work was started while the shelling continued, and on the same day a shell landing on a cellar in Epehy killed 15 men. Even apparently safe shelters were found to be dangerous – a house in Peizière, which was still in relatively good condition, was being used as a Brigade HQ when a quantity of high explosive, as a booby trap, was found hidden under the beams. The building was hastily evacuated.

The Royal Engineers and infantry of the division were very active in improving the defences – digging trenches, connecting posts and setting up wires as the front was by now almost stationary, with the Germans holding the previously prepared main Hindenburg Line – which was now within range of the British artillery – and some outpost positions.

At the northern end of the ridge the village of Villers Guislain was still held and stubbornly defended by the Germans. At dawn on the 14 April the 2nd Devonshires of the 8th Division tried to enter but were prevented from doing so by thick wire surrounding it and heavy machine gun fire from within. They were forced to abandon the attack but returned the following night and cut large gaps in the wire entanglements; the village and the defenders were then heavily shelled. Early in the morning on 18 April the 2nd West Yorkshires walked into the ruins and killed 60 Germans, taking 18 prisoners. British casualties were extremely light, being limited to one man who was reported to be wounded 'in that portion of his anatomy which ought not strictly to have been turned towards the enemy'. [23]

During the approach to Villers Guislain the 8th Division had captured Vaucellete Farm. This farm had housed a large calibre German gun – a railway had been laid to take the gun into the barn – which had fired on the British during the battle of the Somme. A large reinforced concrete bunker had also been built in the farm to protect the gun and crew. The local civilian population had been forced to provide labour for the work early in 1916. The remains of the bunker, now shattered, can still be found by the modern buildings.

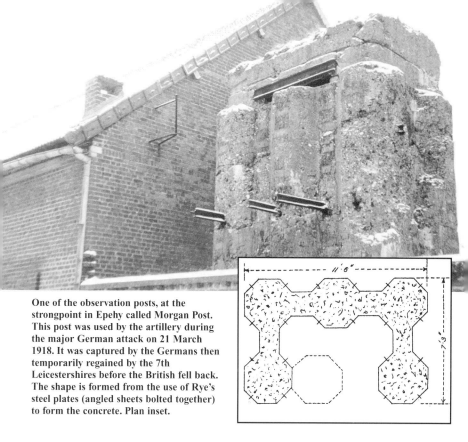

One of the observation posts, at the strongpoint in Epehy called Morgan Post. This post was used by the artillery during the major German attack on 21 March 1918. It was captured by the Germans then temporarily regained by the 7th Leicestershires before the British fell back. The shape is formed from the use of Rye's steel plates (angled sheets bolted together) to form the concrete. Plan inset.

Throughout the summer of 1917 this sector was comparatively quiet, being held by various divisions which were often in need of rest after fighting elsewhere. The defences were maintained and improved and watch was kept on the Germans behind their Hindenburg defences opposite. To improve the observation over the Germans and to protect artillery observers a number of concrete observation towers were built using Rye's steel plates. Two of these observation post towers can still be seen in Epehy and two in Ronssoy.

These villages did not feature in the Cambrai offensive but they played a large part in the German counter offensive of that battle. Within an hour and a half of starting on 30 November 1917 the Germans had captured Villers Guislain, together with almost 60 British field guns and howitzers. They tried to press on and capture Vaucelette Farm but here they met the 1/4th Loyal North Lancashires of the 55th Division who stopped them and then carried out a bold counter-attack before being forced to fall back and consolidate the farm, which they then held with the 6th Queen's Regiment. The 12th Division was forced back through Gauche Wood, which they abandoned to the approaching Germans. The wood was the scene of fierce fighting on the following day, 1 December, when the 2nd Grenadier Guards ran up the slope and at the German machine gunners who had set up there. Casualties were high on both sides but the Grenadiers, reinforced by the 18th Lancers, took control of the wood and established the British front line on its eastern edge.

Other Lancashire battalions of the 55th Division were under pressure in front of Epehy and some ground was given but the line held to the east of the village. The high ground on which Epehy stands remained in British hands through the winter of 1917/18, and was consolidated for defence. During this period a number of concrete artillery posts, using Rye's steel plates, were constructed to give observation of German movements.

When the Germans began their 1918 spring offensive Epehy was held by the 21st Division. The attack began at 7am and the first attempt to take the village was followed by another three hours later. The Germans entered Peizière at 11am but were forced out again after stiff fighting by the 7th Leicesters, aided by two tanks. After clearing the village of Germans the two tanks ran out of petrol attempting to withdraw to their base at Saulcourt to refuel and both were then knocked out by enemy shells while stationary. At 11.58am an officer of the Leicesters sent an urgent request note for replacements: 'I consider two fresh tanks would be most valuable. Sig. Lt. H.R. Horner'[24].

The village was unsuccessfully attacked several times over the next twenty four hours until the Germans, hidden by the morning mist, entered and took Epehy on the morning of 22 March after a heavy artillery bombardment and determined infantry assault on this important high ground. Vaucellete Farm, to the north, was already in German hands, the Northumberland Fusiliers had put up stiff opposition but had been unable to resist the attack.

South of Epehy, the adjoining villages of Lempire and Ronssoy, together with St. Emilie, were defended by the Irishmen of the 16th Division. Shortly before the initial bombardment began the Royal Irish had been ordered forward to man the front defences: they were caught by the barrage and suffered heavy casualties. Nevertheless they put up a spirited fight and delayed the attackers, but were unable to stop them. The Germans had managed to outflank the defenders in the villages and could attack from the east and the south, pockets of Irishmen in strong points were surrounded and most fought on until running out of ammunition. Some were relieved by local counter-attacks, some managed to rejoin their lines but eventually the Germans swept through

Vaucelette Farm was the site of a rail mounted heavy calibre German gun, the crew were housed in a concrete shelter constructed using forced local labour in the spring of 1916. It fired on the British during the Battle of the Somme and the German retirement. The concrete shelter was blown up by the retreating Germans in the spring of 1917, the existing remains show the result of this attempted demolition. The farm was the scene of a determined stand by the 1/4th Loyal North Lancashires on 30 November 1917 and for a time was a British front line position. Another determined stand was made by the 12/13th Northumberland Fusiliers on 21 March 1918; after several hours of stiff fighting with many casualties they were forced out by the Germans who had surrounded the ruins.

The ruins of the Company headquarters of the 2nd Dublins, of the 16th (Irish) Division during the attack on Ronssoy. This position was held until outflanked.

the defences and took the villages. Malassise Farm was strongly defended with machine gun emplacements, trenches and wire entanglements. Garrisoned by the 2nd Royal Munster Fusiliers it held up several waves of attack and inflicted severe casualties: eventually it was overwhelmed, retaken in a counter-attack by a small force led by Lieutenant Cahill, and then lost again. The Irish losses on the day were very high, the killed, wounded and missing included many senior officers. Gauche Wood, garrisoned by the South Africans under Captain Green, was fiercely fought over during the morning but by mid-day the Germans were in occupancy.

THE BATTLE OF EPEHY 18 SEPTEMBER 1918

The British Fourth Army had been pushing the Germans eastwards since the 8th August and in September were once again approaching the outposts of the Hindenburg Line. On 7 September the 12th Division advanced the line to within 1000 metres of Epehy and Peizières. The weather was fine and clear, giving excellent observation for the machine gunners of the Alpine Korps which were defending the village – now a pile of rubble after changing hands several times during earlier battles. The defenders were able to prevent any further advance by the British, who were now pinned down in trenches which had been the Reserve Line in March.

The Queen Victoria's Rifles were ordered to advance the line by pushing forward through the night. At dusk on 7 September patrols of the Q.V.R.s, under Captain Samuelson, pushed forward and captured some of the German front lines. At dawn on 8 September the Q.V.R.s were the most easterly of all British troops in France.

During the day further attempts were made to advance. Patrols succeeded in entering Epehy but were driven out by counter attacks by the Alpine Korps, which also repulsed an attack by the 74th Division, recently arrived from Palestine.

After attacks on 10 September failed it was apparent that the Germans were determined to hold on to the villages and deny the British the benefit of observation over the Hindenburg Line to the east. The British were equally determined to take the high ground and prepared plans for a major assault. Aerial photographs were taken and all defences and strong points noted, troops trained and organised. Planning and preparations took a week and zero hour was set for 5.20am, 18 September. The subsequent action was designated a Battle by the Battle Nomenclature Committee on account of the amount of fighting and the numbers of casualties incurred on both sides. Three divisions were allocated sectors of the front and given objectives. The 18th Division was to capture Ronssoy, then Lempire. The 12th Division was to take Epehy, and the 58th Division was to capture Peizière, at the northern end of Epehy, and Vaucellete Farm. The number of tanks allocated to the attack was kept to eight – the economy of numbers was to save them for the later storming of the main Hindenburg Line.

During the planning the weather had broken and the attack began in very heavy rain – the ground was wet and slippery as the infantry started uphill. There was no preliminary artillery bombardment – the attack was to be a surprise to the defenders. At zero hour a barrage, which moved forward 100 yards each three minutes, began. The 18th Division had great difficulty in moving forward, due to the stout resistance of the German defenders. After six hours of heavy fighting among the ruins they managed to gain the centre of the village and reached the main road – the D58. In the remains of the village hidden machine gun posts fired on the British and caused many casualties. The 6th Northamptonshires were prevented from moving forward by two machine guns until Lance Corporal Lewis crawled up to both emplacements and drove out the machine gun crews with hand grenades, taking a number of prisoners and winning himself a VC. Repeated holdups, largely caused by hidden machine guns, meant that the attack had to be broken off while plans were reorganized. At 5pm the attack was renewed, and Lempire was assaulted at the same time as the 121st German Division launched a counter-attack. The two forces met head on and neither side made progress - the fighting continued amongst the rubble through the evening and night, until on the following morning, 19 September, Lempire was cleared of Germans and consolidated on the next day. At Malassise Farm the 9th Royal Fusiliers had been held up by heavy shelling and were unable to make much progress. The 6th Queen's (Royal West Surrey Regiment) tried the following day; they had difficulties crossing the wire but once that was overcome, in hand-to-hand fighting they took control of the remains of the farm.

Attacking Epehy the Norfolks and Essex fought their way up the western slopes and into the edge of the village, where the 1st Cambridgeshires passed through them to try and capture the strongpoints in the ruins of the village houses. The defences were not in trenches or lines but were concealed in the rubble; strengthened cellars were connected by tunnels and sewers with exits and entrances at manholes. Germans were able to appear behind troops and disappear after firing or throwing bombs, the village was described by one of the attackers as, 'a nest of – surprises'.[25] The tanks which should have assisted had all been ditched or had lost their way, the infantry lost bearings due to the heavy rain and the German shelling which confused their barrage. Close fighting continued through the day as the Bavarian Alpine Korps could not be prised out; a particular strongpoint in the village – named Fishers Keep – took until 7.45pm to subdue, only eleven men of the garrison of 46 remained alive and unwounded. The struggle went on into the evening; in torrential rain the eastern edge of the village slowly fell into British control and it was midnight before the last houses were cleared. The Germans were edged down the eastern slopes over the next few days.

The 58th Division, attacking at the northern end of the village, had been successful and the 2/2nd Londons had almost cleared Peizière by mid morning. Many prisoners were taken together with large numbers of machine guns and mortars.

EPEHY TODAY

In Epehy there are two British observation posts, named Morgan Post and Cullen Post, constructed using Rye's plates, angled metal sheets which were specially made for this purpose. These were used by the British on 21 March 1918 although morning mist reduced their vision. During the British attack on 18 September 1918, they were the only standing constructions. Two similar structures still exist in Ronssoy, although one is hidden from view as a barn was later rebuilt around it. On the eastern edge of Ronssoy – adjacent to the new civilian cemetery, marked 31 on the map – is a British forward dug-out, now partly filled with rubbish. This dug-out was the H.Q. of a Company of the 2nd Dublins when they were attacked on the morning of 21 March 1918, and fought fiercely before being outflanked. The remains of the 1916 German heavy gun emplacement – still evident from the mass concrete – survive at Vaucelette Farm [**no. 32 on map**].

In Gauche Wood, which changed hands several times and was for a time the British front line, and was heavily shelled by both sides, the remains of several temporary corrugated iron shelters can be found. Lancashire Trench, which was for a while the forward defences held by the South Africans, can still be traced.

Several British artillery observation posts, built using the same system of steel Rye's plates, can be found in Epehy and Lempire. All were used during the defence of the village in March 1918.

This area was the southern sector of the planned gains for the opening part of the attack on 20 November 1917 which became the Battle of Cambrai. Whilst the planners hoped for a major breakthrough – the plans included the encirclement of Cambrai by the cavalry, which was to break the railways and other lines of communication in addition to capturing a major German headquarters on the outskirts of the town – their expectations were less grand whilst some contingencies, such as the need for reserves, were not allowed for.

The opening part of the attack included the use of tanks, which were to operate for the first time on a landscape chosen by the Tank Corps. The gently rolling chalk hill grassland was thought to be ideal, being very little fought over and relatively unscarred by shell fire. The German trenches to be traversed were known to be deep and wide, so arrangements were made to provide the tanks with fascines, bundles of wood which could be dropped into the trench by the tank before crossing. The production of these bridges, manufactured by two tanks tightening the bundles with steel chains, required much material – on this sector 216 tanks each required a fascine which could be dropped into position only once. Three divisions were to carry out the opening attack with a fourth, the 29th Division, being used to exploit the initial gains. The 12th (Eastern) Division were on the right, they were to storm the Hindenburg Line in front of Bonavis then capture Lateau Wood. Twelve of the 72 tanks allotted to them, from F Tank Battalion, were to proceed up the Roman road to Masnières, the N44, and capture the canal bridge there, allowing the cavalry to cross, and others were to stay with the infantry and clear and consolidate the rear defence lines. On the left was the 20th (Light) Division which was to capture the high ground of Welsh Ridge, on their left; on the other side of the railway line the 6th Division were to proceed to Marcoing, where their tanks, B Battalion, were to take and hold the canal and rail bridges there.

Zero hour was 6.20am on 20 November. A dull and overcast morning started quietly as troops and tanks had moved to the start lines in great

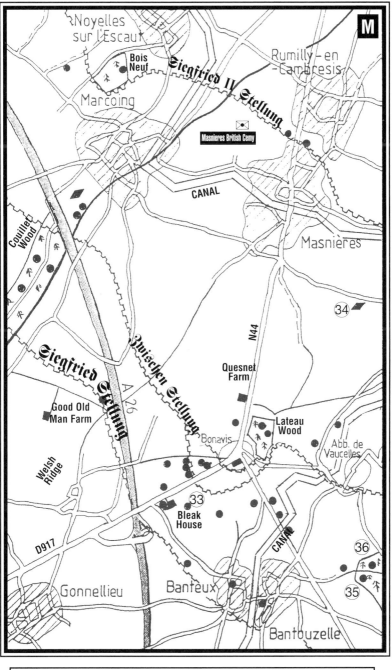

M

Noyelles sur l'Escaut

Bois Neuf

Siegfried II Stellung

Rumilly-en-Cambresis

Marcoing

Masnieres British Cemy

CANAL

Couillet Wood

Masnières

34

Siegfried Stellung

Zwischen Stellung

N44

A 26

Quesnet Farm

Good Old Man Farm

Lateau Wood

Bonavis

Abb. de Vaucelles

Welsh Ridge

33

Bleak House

D917

CANAL

36

Gonnellieu

Banteux

35

Bantouzelle

⊔⊓⊔⊓⊔⊓ Main trench line	● Existing structure, British or German, e.g. pill box
◤ Site of interest	
+ Memorial	⊠ Cemeteries

Abschnitt V1

German trench map of the Hindenburg Line defences in front of Bonavis and Lateau Wood. The support line had originally been intended as the front line until the scheme was adjusted by Colonel von Lossberg to include the high ground on which Le Pavé Farm stands. Many of the command bunkers and observation posts remain.

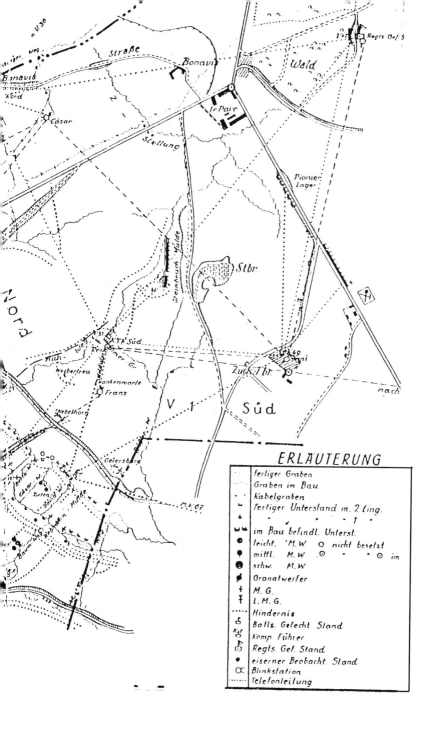

ERLÄUTERUNG

	fertiger Graben
	Graben im Bau
	Kabelgraben
	fertiger Unterstand m. 2 Eing.
	im Bau befindl. Unterst.
	leicht. M.W. nicht besetzt
	mittl. M.W. im
	schw. M.W.
	Granatwerfer
	M. G.
	L. M. G.
	Hindernis
	Batls. Gefecht. Stand
	Komp. Führer
	Regts. Gef. Stand
	eiserner Beobacht. Stand
	Blinkstation
	Telefonleitung

By the small road from Banteaux to the motorway junction can be found this infantry command post and light signal station (*Blinkstelle*), sending and receiving signals used for communication. Shaped like a house, and close behind the front trench of the Hindenburg Line, it is completely out of sight of the British lines on the other side of the high ground.

One of the front line observation posts (no. 33 on map). The thick steel periscope hatch gave excellent views over the British lines. This was later used as a strongpoint by the 9th Royal Fusiliers, they held out here whilst besieged by the Germans but were forced to surrender.

secrecy. At the same time as they moved forward a very heavy artillery barrage opened up on the German trenches, strongpoints, roads and battery positions. The 12th Division troops swept over their first objectives. The ridge of high ground between Banteux and Bonavis, and the stretch of the main Hindenburg Line on it, was captured by the 5th Royal Berkshires and the 9th Essex with the 7th Suffolks; many of the tanks supporting them broke down or got stuck in the sunken lane between Gonnelieu and Banteux (the D96). Sonnet Farm – which stood where the motorway slip roads now are - fell to the 8th Royal Fusiliers, although serious opposition came from Bleak House, where the derelict brickworks now stands. This stood immediately behind the main trench and was an important part of the defences. Remains of the strong point – a concrete bunker – which was taken by a joint infantry and tank attack – still stands in the farm yard. Nearby is a concrete observation post.

The house at Le Pavé contained machine guns which slowed the advance until they were knocked out by tanks and the Germans surrendered. Pam Pam Farm (the site is now occupied by a restaurant) was a strong position with several machine guns in concrete shelters, the 6th Buffs overcame these with the aid of tanks and then went on to tackle the buildings at Bonavis Farm, on the corner.

Progress to the north of the Gouzeaucourt-Bonavis (D917) road had also been to schedule, although a party of Germans put up a spirited resistance at le Quesnet farm. The 6th Royal West Kents attacked the farm but suffered losses in doing so, after entering the farm under the command of Captain Dove they were overpowered, captured and taken prisoner by the Germans. However the Germans were forced to retire and abandon the farm by attacks on their flanks and during this retirement Captain Dove managed to escape, taking three Germans away as prisoners. Most of the fighting was now centred around and within Lateau Wood, which had to be captured to deny the Germans observation over the other parts of the battlefield. Hidden in the wood were several batteries of guns, some of heavy calibre, and some machine gun positions. The wood had been the original siting of the Hindenburg Line before the scheme was completed and it contained many dugouts and a command post. Defence of the wood was very patchy. The 6th Royal West Kents easily took the northern part of it, reporting later: 'enemy taken completely by surprise and appeared utterly demoralised'[26].

Sharp fighting took place elsewhere in the wood before it was in British hands, the infantry assisted by tanks of C Battalion, who lost many tanks to German gunners. By 11am the wood was cleared of

In Lateau Wood still stands the artillery observation post used by the Germans during the British assault. The MarinKorps who built it added, in German, the inscription over the sight embrasure:

'In greatest need was this built here, for a hero's death I greatly fear,
23.4.17. M.K. 19'

The post was captured by the Royal West Kents but lost during the German counter offensive. It has been tilted by a later explosion but is otherwise still in good condition, including inscription.

Germans and the southern edge became the British front line. The 12th Division had captured five officers, 378 other ranks, eight heavy howitzers, eight field guns and mortars, and 22 machine guns: their own losses were described as 'comparatively the lightest we had experienced, 144 killed, 841 wounded, 160 missing.'[27]

Masnières village was a German garrison for this sector of the line but also held a large civilian population, mainly women and children. As the British attack was unexpected they were as surprised as the Germans but were delighted to have the chance of freedom. Lieutenant Duval, an interpreter with the 20th Division, arranged for them to be evacuated away from the artillery fire, led away down the Cambrai road (the N44) singing the 'Marsellaise'.

The main road bridge in Masnières village was important to both sides: the Germans wanted to deny its use to the British, who had made plans to capture and hold it, and were in the act of blowing it up when the first British troops entered the village at about noon. The attempt at demolition was not wholly successful although it was visibly weakened and the tanks hesitated before trying to cross. At 12.40am, with the

Most of the heavily shelled farmland was levelled and ploughed following the war, and little is left to give an idea of it's former condition. A rare example is to be found between Masnières and les-Rues-des-Vignes; this ground was the furthest extent of the British advance on the opening day of the Battle of Cambrai. Captured by the 20th (Light) Division it was held as the front line for ten days, being lost on the German counter-attack on 30 November.

Germans massing and manning rifle and machine gun positions to cover the crossing, a tank of F Battalion, commanded by Lieutenant Edmundson, approached the damaged bridge and started to cross, under heavy fire. The tank got half way across before the bridge collapsed; the crew managed to escape under fire but the tank was stuck and when the bridge was again in German hands they used the tank as support for a new bridge. Several infantry battalions tried to force a crossing but were unable to do so in any numbers. The 1st Essex made repeated crossings and tried to clear the Germans from the houses in the village but did not get as far as the trenches of the Masnières-Beaurevoir Line on the northern outskirts. They did manage to hold the bridgehead and, together with the 2nd Hampshires and the 4th Worcestershires, made a determined effort during the night of 20 November to push the Germans back. In heavy rain they gained the trenches of the Masnières - Beaurevoir Line but the Germans held fast in front of Rumilly-en-Cambrésis. The British planners felt they had insufficient reserves and tanks to press further and so gave orders for the troops to consolidate their gains and prepare defensive measures in case of a German counter-attack. The British front line was formed from the German trenches, and stretched from the eastern side of Masnières, half way to Crévecoeur, across the Cambrai road to where the Newfoundlanders had also won a length of the German trenches. The limit of their progress – the rear trench of the Masnières-Beaurevoir Line – is today marked by the Caribou Memorial. Close to this is a German command bunker captured and used by them as a front line post.

The German bunker of the Masnières-Beaurevoir Line at Masnières was the limit of the Newfoundlanders progress during the battle and became their front line post.

British troops spent the next week strengthening defences whilst the Generals tried to decide whether the Germans were likely to launch a determined counter-attack or were too weakened and without sufficient reserves. Uncertainty reigned until 8am on 30 November. The first to know of the attack were the 5th Royal Berkshires, holding a front line post at the quarry in front of Banteux. Germans of the 109th Fusiliers swarmed out of Banteux: the Berkshires were forced to concede ground but then won it back, only to have it taken from them again. More Germans, who had formed up around the Grenouillere bridge (several of their concrete shelters are still to be found around the bridge, although the ones in the Grainor works are on private land) attacked the 7th East Surreys who held the farm on the road junction (Bonavis) and Pam Pam Farm. The East Surreys were forced to retire beyond Pam Pam Farm under a concerted thrust, but then they regrouped and forced the Germans back over the main road and retook both farms. Another German attack followed and Pam Pam Farm fell, the East Surreys in Bonavis Farm were now surrounded but fought on until, at 1.30pm, with only ten men remaining unwounded, they ran out of ammunition. The commanding officer, Lieutenant-Colonel Baldwin, decided to surrender. Meanwhile the 6th Royal West Kents had been forced out of Lateau Wood by Germans who bombed their way up the Hindenburg Support trench from Vaucelles Abbey, which had been used as a supply dump until then. After Lateau Wood fell the Germans attacked the 8th and 9th Royal Fusiliers who held positions around Bleak House, after an artillery bombardment which included gas and smoke shells. Most of the main road was soon in German hands although they did not win it easily; several counter attacks were made by the Royal Fusiliers, one of which was lead by Lieutenant-Colonel Elliott-Cooper who rallied troops

Neville Bowes Elliott-Cooper VC

and forced the Germans back over the road towards Banteux. Elliott-Cooper was severely wounded but, seeing they were greatly outnumbered, ordered his men to retire, knowing he would be captured. He was awarded the VC for his gallantry but later died as a prisoner in Germany. Bleak House itself – originally part of the main Hindenburg Line – was a position with three strong points around it. This was manned by D Company of the 9th Royal Fusiliers who were surrounded and beseiged by the Germans. They held out all day while several unsuccessful attempts at relief were made, but the survivors were forced to surrender during the evening.

The Germans were now in possession of the high ground of Bonavis Ridge and their front line ran approximately parallel with the

Gouzeaucourt road. They had also forced the British back over the Masnières road (the N44), as far back as the Hindenburg Support Line. Low flying aircraft bombed and machine gunned the British trenches and posts and the German infantry advanced in a succession of from eight to twelve waves. The 10th Rifle Brigade headquarters was overwhelmed and the few staff who survived were taken prisoner. The British troops were pushed back to Welsh Ridge but managed to stem the tide there and denied the high ground to the Germans.

Masnières village was now under threat from the south and was also being attacked from the north and east. A complete Field Company of Royal Engineers (about 200 men) were sleeping after night work when the Germans attacked, were literally caught napping and taken prisoner.

Robert Gee VC

Infantry battalions of the Lancashire Fusiliers, Royal Fusiliers, Middlesex Regiment and the Royal Guernsey Light Infantry held Masnières against repeated German attacks, after desperate street fighting amid the ruins they held on. A party of Germans set up a machine gun on the edge of the village but Captain Gee rushed the position, shot the crew with his revolver and turned the machine gun on to more Germans who were advancing. For this bravery and other deeds on the day he was awarded the VC. Although Masnières was still in British hands it was surrounded on three sides and the following night, under cover of darkness, the village was evacuated and left to the Germans.

Arthur Moore Lascelles VC

The British front line now ran in front of Marcoing. On 3 December the Germans again attacked: the 14th Durham Light Infantry and the 1st King's Shropshire Light Infantry were trapped in trenches in the angle of the canal, heavy fighting raged, trenches were lost and regained in counter attacks (Captain Lascelles was awarded the VC for his leadership in rallying forces whilst wounded, and escaping from captivity) although the defenders were eventually forced to retire back over the canal, crossing at the railway bridge. Early in the following morning the Royal Engineers blew up all the canal bridges around Marcoing, using German explosives. The advancing Germans were fought to a standstill at the canal. On the following day, 4 December, orders were given to prepare for the evacuation of Marcoing, to be preceded by the demolition of dugouts, withdrawal of guns, and the preparation of booby traps.

Following the British evacuation of this area and the reversion to German occupancy, it became a quieter area for almost a year: in

156

September, 1918 the Germans were again on the defensive behind the Hindenburg Line and the British were about to attack and push them further eastwards. During the afternoon of 28 September the Hindenburg line defences on the high ground of Welsh Ridge was stormed and taken by the 8th Manchesters and the 8th Lancashire Fusiliers. Resistance had initially been stiff but this soon weakened and many prisoners were taken: 'so thoroughly beaten and so glad to be out of the fighting, that they took charge of themselves and marched into captivity without escort.'[28]

Marcoing was entered and the canal crossed by the 2/4th Hampshires, followed by the 5th Duke of Wellingtons, who crossed under cover of Lewis gun fire from the remaining houses on the west bank. Masnières fell easily, as did Rumilly, which had been impossible to enter the previous November.

Lateau Wood was entered by the 1st Auckland and 2nd Wellington Battalions of New Zealanders, after some heavy fighting, on 29 September, capturing the bunkers taken and then lost by the Royal West Kents in 1917. The following day the New Zealanders tried to cross the canal at Vaucelles but were prevented from doing so by German machine guns around the Abbey, the buildings and grounds of which had been used as a main supply dump. On the same day the 5th Division was stopped in Banteux by machine gun fire from a pill box which still stands on the far side of the bridge to Bantouzelle.

The pill box covering the canal bridge at Banteaux. The German machine gun crew prevented troops of the 5th Division from crossing the bridge in September 1918.

On 5 October, 1918 the Germans retired from the east bank of the canal, allowing the British to cross on improvised bridges and small rafts left behind by the Germans. The fighting then passed to the Beaurevoir Line to the east.

THE AREA TODAY

Many of the 1917/18 defences fought over can still be found. In Banteux village is a good example of camouflage, the concrete pill box built into the garden wall, with its machine gun aperture, can be difficult to spot. The pill box which caused problems to the British on 30 September 1918 is still to be seen beneath the house facing the canal bridge. To the east of Bantouzelle, on the edge of Vaucelles Wood, is a large command post concreted into the hillside [**no. 35 on map**] and a large, double chambered underground supply dump [**no. 36 on map**]. This was the end of a light railway, hoops in the wall were probably for tethering pack mules.

Several bunkers can be found in the fields between Banteux and Bonavis, one bears the inscription:

'Erbaut in Sept 1917 von III/P.K.'

Lateau Wood contains a concrete observation post with a heartfelt inscription [see photograph] and the remains of the command centre for this sector. In a small copse a few hundred metres eastwards along the Hindenburg Support Line, close to the D103, is the broken

One of the double chambered bunkers still to be found, used as the terminal of a trench railway.

A German command bunker with two large chambers, built into the hill in the wood to the east of Bantouzelle.

remains of another underground centre. In the fields between Bonavis and the A26 are a number of pill boxes and bunkers captured by the 12th Division on the opening day of the Battle of Cambrai. The high ground of Welsh Ridge, where the Germans made a stand against the 42nd Division on 28 September 1918, is a bleak and featureless landscape crossed by few tracks. The 10th Manchesters gained a foothold on the ridge, on the summit of which stood Good Old Man Farm. Here the 8th Lancashire Fusiliers overtook the strong point and took control of the crest. Today the farmhouse, later rebuilt, again stands derelict.

Just north of Masnières, close to the Canadian Memorial, are two bunkers which were occupied by the Newfoundlanders and then used by them as front line command centres.

Vaucelles Abbey had been a stores dump for the Germans, they set fire to it when retreating in 1918, the main hall was not rebuilt and still carries the scars of the fighting.

N
BONY AND VENDHUILE

The Germans, falling back to the Hindenburg Line near Vendhuile in September 1918, were chased by the 12th (Eastern) Division; first to arrive at the Canal de St Quentin in Vendhuile were the 6th East Kents and the 6th Royal West Kents. The Germans retired to the Hindenburg Line beyond the ruins of Vendhuile, leaving them to the British, but did not allow them to cross the Canal.

The Americans of the 27th and 30th American Divisions, attached to the Australian Corps, were to carry out the difficult task of dislodging the Germans from the main Hindenburg Line between Bellicourt and Vendhuile, centred on Bony. The attack began at 4.50am on 29 September; before they could reach the Hindenburg Line the Americans had first to take the outpost line which included some strong positions where, it was expected, the Germans would put up determined resistance. Facing the 27th American Division were three such major obstacles: the Knoll (named *Sappenberg* by the Germans), Gillemont Farm and Quennemont Farm, each strongly fortified and armed with field guns, heavy machine guns, anti-tank rifles and infantry. Machine guns were also distributed around the forward and rear trench lines.

The 27th American Division had 34 Mark V tanks, manned by the 301st American Tank Battalion, allocated to it. The use of tanks was not successful, some were blown up as they crossed a forgotten British mine field laid in 1917, many received direct hits from artillery and anti-tank rifles, and seven ditched.

Seven tanks got to within a hundred metres of Gillemont Farm but were put out of action by the German defenders; only one tank succeeded in crossing the trenches of the Hindenburg Line on this front.

The doughboys of the 107th Infantry Regiment – New Yorkers, formerly the 7th Infantry, National Guard – came under intense fire from the German positions as soon as the attack started over the open ground. Depleted numbers reached The Knoll, where they engaged Germans of the 54th Division: 'fighting for the possession of The Knoll was most costly, but the men hammered on. Prisoners were few, as

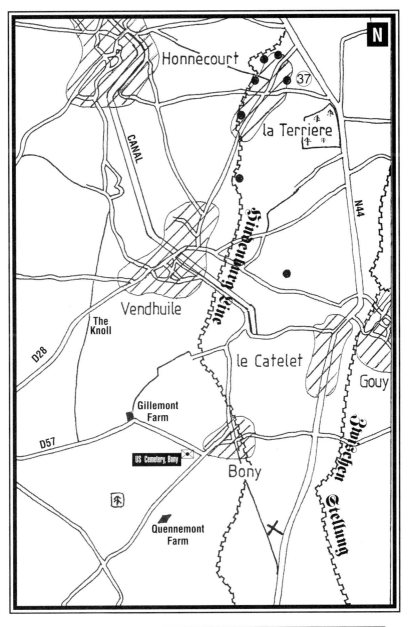

hand-to-hand conflicts were necessary before the trenches were finally cleared.'[29]

The Germans launched a counter attack to regain the position, the Americans fought it off and did the same a second time, but a third attack left The Knoll (*Sappenberg*) back in German hands.

Gillemont Farm fell to the remnants of troops who had been decimated by machine guns:

'The enemy contested the advance and were killed as each trench was reached. Few surrendered. In the ruins, in hedges, in every copse were concealed Boche machine guns, and as the men charged up the slope they received this murderous fire full in their faces. It was rifles, bayonets and bombs against machine guns. The units hurled themselves in one last assault upon Gillemont Farm and its network of defenses and were met by an increased intensity of fire from the desperate Hun garrison. Through the smoking ruins of the Farm, over machine guns spitting death to the last, bombing pillboxes and dugouts, they emerged from a hedge on the other side."[30]

Most of the officers leading the attack on the Farm were killed, including Second Lieutenant Rambo, who was given a Citation for 'courage and fearlessness in leading his platoon forward in the attack on the Hindenburg Line.'

A number of men of the 3rd battalion of the 107th Regiment worked their way past the north of Gillemont and reached the Hindenburg Line front and support trenches in front of Gouy, where they were cut off as Germans were able to appear behind them, emerging from the many tunnels and inter-connected dugouts. Air patrols confirmed the Americans position in the Hindenburg Line but the surrounded troops were not seen again.

Second Lieutenant Rambo, the New Yorker who was killed at Gillemont Farm after carrying out acts of bravery for which he was awarded a Citation.

The force of the American attack had been expended on the three strongpoints, and lack of fighting experience had led to incomplete mopping up leaving many posts and trenches overlooked and passed. Bony and the Hindenburg Line were still in German hands and the 3rd Australian Division, which was to have passed through the Americans, had to capture Gillemont and Quennemont Farms before proceeding. This they managed to do, but they could not reach Bony. Armoured cars and whippet tanks tried to enter the village from the Hargicourt Road but were unable to, some were lost to anti-tank fire and the others retired.

The Australians made plans for another attack on the following day: as Bellicourt had been taken on the previous day they intended working northwards up the Hindenburg Line. Starting at 6am they bombed and bayonetted their way up the trenches but the Germans resisted and progress was slow, machine guns hindered movement and by nightfall they had only a toe-hold on the southern outskirts of Bony. The struggle continued through the night and into the following morning; at noon on 1 October the Australians were finally in and through the ruins of Bony and the Hindenburg Line.

Le Catelet was cleared of Germans on 3 October by the 2nd Royal Munster Fusiliers of the 50th Division, who were to clear their left flank while they took Prospect Hill to the east.

The Germans still held out on the east bank of the canal at Vendhuile, where the Hindenburg Line ran up to the high ground of La Terrière, which was a strongly held position. During the early hours of 5 October patrols of the 50th (Northumbrian) Division crossed the canal and found the Germans had vacated the part of Vendhuile on that side of the Canal, and the trenches up to La Terrière were empty. The Northumbrians handed them over to the Welshmen of the 38th Division.

La Terrière, standing on high ground overlooking the Canal and land to the east, was a strongpoint of the Hindenburg Line with many concrete artillery bunkers and pill boxes. This one, in a small quarry (now disused but adjoining a private house) was probably for the protection of an artillery battery crew.

THE AREA TODAY

The village of Bony and the surrounding area give little indication of the events which resulted in the American Cemetery. Gillemont Farm, where many of the New Yorkers were killed, was rebuilt after the war and is now a large and sprawling agricultural industry unit. Quennemont Farm, which the Americans were unable to capture, was not rebuilt and the site is occupied by a radio mast. The track leading to the farm is still identifiable. The copse nearby, Quennet Copse, from where German machine gunners mowed down many Americans, still has much broken ground from shelling and assorted metal pieces lying around in the undergrowth.

The high ground of The Knoll, the third major obstacle faced by the Americans, is arable farmland and a blank, featureless expanse from which valleys run down to the canal and Vendhuile.

Around La Terrière are still a number of remnants of the Hindenburg defence line, deserted by the Germans as the British approached.

The success of the American attack on Bony was thwarted by Germans emerging from dugouts and tunnels once the Americans had passed. The network of tunnels was connected by a number of exits in houses, farm buildings and bunkers. Most of those around Bony have been cleared and filled and are difficult to find but a number can be found in and around Bellicourt. The one below was reached and passed by the 30th American Division but then Germans emerged and captured the Americans. The entrance to the tunnels from the bunker has been bricked up to prevent entry.

BELLICOURT AND BELLENGLISE

By 4 April 1917 the 59th, 61st and other British divisions had followed and pushed the retreating Germans almost to the Hindenburg Line, which in this sector ran along the eastern side of the Canal de St. Quentin up to Bellicourt where it swung westwards out in front of the village. The Germans were not yet ready to fall right back and started to put up much stiffer resistance where they thought it in their interests to do so. Some British gains were lost to German counter-attacks but these were recaptured and more ground was made as further attacks were pressed.

On the morning of 15 April, 1917, the Bantams of the 35th Division took the area in front of and around Pontruet and on the following morning they found that the Germans had evacuated the village. By late April all of the ground fronting the outpost line, which ran 1500-2000 metres in front of the main Hindenburg Line, was in British hands and the enemy defences were within range of field artillery. With the Germans now well established behind their main defence lines the pursuit was over and the sector became quiet. Whilst further north, at Bullecourt and Arras, and later on at Cambrai, fighting continued, the front here settled into a daily pattern: artillery shelling and sniping was fairly continuous and night patrolling in No Mans Land was risky but trench life was routine and orderly. A quiet summer and winter saw many divisions,usually resting and refitting after fighting elsewhere, holding the line. The Germans also had a quiet time; Ernst Jünger of the 73rd Hanoverian Fusilier Regiment recalled staying at Riqueval Farm in May, spending time sunbathing and boating on the canal[31].

With the expectations of a 1918 spring offensive by the Germans it was decided to reorganise the defences which had been allowed to deteriorate and strengthen the sector for the attack. At the end of February the 66th Division, which had spent the last few months in the Ypres area after taking part in the capture of Passchaendale, took over the northern part, but were not happy with the state of the trenches and defence systems. The Royal Engineers of the division recorded that:

'work handed over included a golf course, an officers club with garden and a theatre but the defences which every one wanted to see were difficult to find. The latter included an old and decayed outpost line – the same as was first taken up last year – a poorly sited and made main line of resistance.'[32]

Some trenches were found to be dug to only 1 foot 6 inches deep, with few decent shelters and roads in a poor state of repair. The Royal Engineers and infantry working parties of the Lancashire regiments then spent the first few weeks of March hurriedly digging and building defences.

The 24th Division in front of Bellenglise to the south were also hard at work digging and improving trenches and strongpoints.

With the increased expectancy that the German thrust would include this part of the line both divisions had the dual task of improving defences and arranging and practising manning them. Troops spent the days preparing defences and the nights on alert and at their alarm stations. On the night of 19 March a German N.C.O. deserted into the 66th Division lines and told of the impending attack, timed for 48 hours later. The two divisions were then on full alert for the assault when it did come.

21 MARCH 1918

At about 4 o'clock on the morning of 21 March a terrific bombardment opened up on the British positions. Gun battery positions, divisional and battalion headquarters, telephone exchanges, trench lines and strong points were all shelled with a mixture of high explosive and gas shells. A heavy fog hung in the air which mixed with the gas, putting gun crews out of action and disrupting communications. The fog had thinned only slightly when, at 9.40am, the German assault infantry appeared out of the mist, pouring out of the Hindenburg Line and over their outpost line to begin their Spring offensive.

The 24th and 66th Divisions were overwhelmed by numbers, being attacked by nine German divisions. Battalions in the front line trenches were swept aside as the troops were either killed or taken prisoner. Strong points in the support and reserve lines put up fierce resistance, causing many casualties in the German ranks, these obstacles to the advance were either surrounded and bombed into submission or by-passed to be dealt with later by moppers-up. Pontruet fell in the middle of the morning and by mid-day the fighting was intense over most of the front; the Germans had infiltrated the British defences in many areas but were held up by isolated pockets of resistance. The 8th

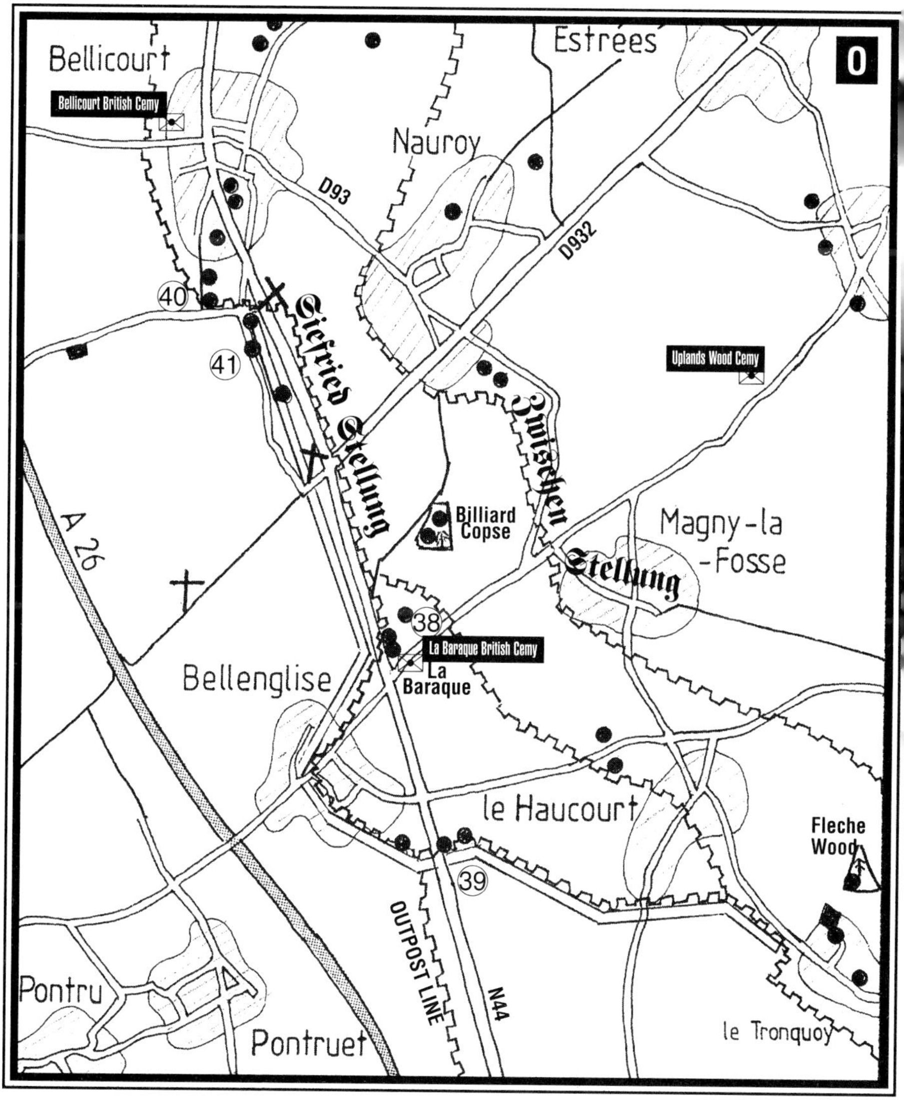

0
Bellicourt
Bellicourt British Cemy
Estrées
Nauroy
D93
D932
40
41
Siegfried Stellung
Zwischen Stellung
Uplands Wood Cemy
Billiard Copse
Magny-la
-Fosse
38
La Baraque British Cemy
La Baraque
Bellenglise
A 26
le Haucourt
Fleche Wood
39
OUTPOST LINE
N44
Pontru
Pontruet
le Tronquoy

Main trench line	Existing structure, British or German, e.g. pill box
Site of interest	Cemeteries
Memorial	

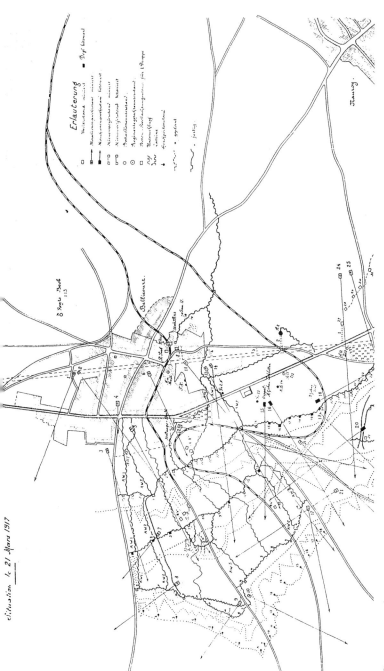

German map of the Hindenburg Line defences around the tunnel entrance. Most of the machine gun emplacements and bunkers still exist; some are easily found but others are buried and identifiable only by small patches of coarse grass and weeds.

168

The entrance to the canal tunnel or souterrain after its capture, with the view today (inset). This was an important part of the defences and housed many German troops in barges. The entrance was protected by carefully sited machine gun positions, many of which gave major problems to the Americans who were to capture it. A small doorway just inside the tunnel mouth still leads to the hidden machine gun post, on a platform inside (now in a delapidated and dangerous condition). The loop hole still exists but is nowadays hidden by the trees on the left embankment.

Queen's, of the 24th Division, put up a stout resistance in Le Verguier, the Germans made attempts to enter the village from the east, the north and the south, shelling the village and making infantry assaults which were fought off with heavy losses on both sides. The remnant of the 8th Queen's – by now a much reduced force – evacuated the village on the following morning to avoid capture by the Germans who by then encircled them.

Villeret was garrisoned by the 2/6th Manchesters who defended the village stubbornly, the Germans tried to pass around them but were unable to do so due to the machine gun fire from within the village defences. The defenders to the north were not so much of a problem to the Germans who captured the headquarters of the 2/8th Lancashire Fusiliers before the occupants realised the attack had even started.

By the afternoon of 22 March both divisions had retired to the west and the Hindenburg Line was once again a quiet area, and was not to see further action until the Germans fell back to the position in the autumn.

SEPTEMBER 1918

By 18 September the Germans had again been pushed back and were about to be attacked by the pursuing British. They were occupying the ground won on the first day of the spring offensive but were now on the defensive. Their front line used many of the trenches and strong points which had been dug by the British and they were hurriedly reorganising themselves to ward off the expected attack. Their intention was to maintain this line as a first defence to prevent their enemy from approaching their main defence - the trenches of the Hindenburg Line.

The attack was to be carried out by the Australians. The 1st and 4th Australian Divisions were allotted nine tanks to assist them; the attack began without a preliminary artillery bombardment, to give a degree of surprise, although once the attack began an intense machine-gun barrage started which moved forward with the infantry. A novel method of use of machine guns in three echelons: 'barrage' (64 guns), 'support' (32 guns) and 'forward' (32 guns) in addition to those used to support the advancing infantry meant that bullets rained down on the defenders and were instrumental in the success of the attack.

James Park Woods VC

Le Verguier was cleared of Germans after they had put up a determined defence of the village; two Australians (Pte. Woods, for capturing and holding a strong point, and Sgt. Sexton, for capturing a field gun and several machine guns by firing a Lewis gun from the hip) were awarded VC's for bravery around the village. Villeret was cleared by the 1st Australian Brigade with the help of tanks from B Company of the 2nd Tank Battalion; the 1st Brigade also cleared the maze of trenches around Cologne Farm, which was known to be strongly wired and defended. The 14th Battalion obtained a footing in the outer defences of the Hindenburg Line and bombed its way up the trench to consolidate the position. Resistance stiffened, and it was decided to await until dark and then renew the attack.

Maurice Vincent Sexton VC

The Australians were given a hot meal and a rest, and ordered to attack again at 11pm. By 1am all objectives had been taken and most of the outer defences of the Hindenburg Line – including the March 1918 British front line which had been incorporated by the Germans – was in British hands. During the day's fighting the Australians had taken 4,243 prisoners, and captured 87 field guns and over 300 machine guns. The stage was now set for the assault on the main Hindenburg Line, which was expected to be an extremely difficult task.

The section from the south side of Bellenglise village to north of the canal bridge at Riqueval was allotted to three battalions of the 46th (North Midland) Division. The main German trenches ran along the eastern edge of the canal, which meant that the attackers would be under fire whilst descending the steep embankment and crossing the canal. The Hindenburg Line had been sited here with this intention. At 5.50am on 29 September the attack began. The 1/6th South Staffords were to cross the canal and capture Bellenglise. At the start the light was good but as the troops set off a fog came down, which, mixed with the smoke of the artillery barrage, made it impossible to see. This meant that some attackers had difficulty finding their way but also obscured them from the German machine gunners. The water level in the canal was low but still too deep to wade. Some officers swam across with lines, some troops crossed on rafts made of cork and petrol tins.

The first of the South Staffords across the canal met with determined resistance but after this was overcome many of the Germans surrendered freely. Several hundred Germans had taken shelter in the tunnel which was known to exist under Bellenglise. Before they had time to resist they were taken prisoner by a small party of British troops. The tunnel had been intended as a shelter but turned out to be a trap for the defenders. The village defences were then mopped up one by one and the 1/6th Sherwood Foresters passed through to attack Lehaucourt to the east at noon. By now the fog had cleared and they came under fire from German field and machine guns which held up progress until Lieutenant-Colonel Vann, a clergyman of the Church of England prior to joining the Army, led the line forward. He rushed one field gun, shooting one gunner with a revolver and clubbing two others, enabling the attack to continue. He was awarded the VC for gallantry during this action.

Bernard William Vann VC

The stretch of canal from the northern edge of Bellenglise to just beyond the Riqueval Bridge was to be crossed by the 1/5th South Staffords and the 1/6th North Staffords. On 28 September, the day before the planned attack, the Germans carried out a pre-emptive strike;

The view from the bridge at Riqueval, where the canal narrows. This was the northern limit of the 46th Division attack on 29 September 1918. The difficulties facing the troops, who, once they had captured the trenches at the top of the left (west) bank, can be seen: they had to descend the embankment, which was wired, and then either swim or place bridges across the water, whilst the Germans waited on the other side. The morning mist, combined with smoke from the artillery barrage, greatly reduced the effectiveness of the defender's machine gun and artillery observation.

Most of the machine guns covering the Canal were difficult to identify. This one, on the bend 380 metres south of the Tunnel, was built into the embankment stone facing, the modern signpost covers the loop hole. A small doorway (normally blocked) to the left leads into the position and a connecting tunnel system which was electrically lit. This gave a good field of fire over the section crossed by the Staffordshires but fortunately morning mist obscured the view.

for six hours they pressed the British front line, and 'fighting was very severe indeed.'[33]

Eventually they were beaten off and the Staffords were able to form up for their own attack. In addition to his normal load of a rifle and bayonet, 120 rounds of ammunition, two bombs, entrenching tools, Box Respirator and mess tin, unconsumed portion of the day's rations and full water bottle, each man carried a lifebelt. Portable bridging material, collapsible boats and scaling ladders were also to be carried by designated troops.

The outpost line, which ran along the western bank of the canal, was taken without any difficulty, and several hundred prisoners were taken. There was some resistance from the main defence line on the eastern bank; German machine gunners took a heavy toll as the men crossed the canal although the low visibility, caused by fog, helped reduce casualties.

An hour after zero all troops, lead by officers, were across the canal and tackling the defender's machine and field guns. Resistance crumbled as the Staffords worked their way up the canal bank and into the trenches on the top of the slope, they:

> '... found themselves in the midst of bewildered parties of the enemy. One Officer and his orderly captured 75 Bosche. Cases of parties of Germans, 11, 20 and 30 strong surrendering to individuals was common.'[34]

The bridge at Riqueval carried the old Roman road (named Watling Street by the British) which ran between Vermand and Bavay. A main supply route used by the Germans, they wished to deny it to the British and defended it with a machine gun post on the west bank and prepared it for demolition. Captain Charlton of the 1/6th North Staffords and an Engineer detachment rushed and overpowered the machine gun crew, then raced a party of German pioneers to the fuses. Four pioneers were shot, the charges thrown into the canal and the bridge was safe.

By mid-morning all of the east canal bank section of the Hindenburg Line was captured and the troops moved on to other objectives. The 1/5th South Staffords captured the German command post in the concrete shelters at la Baraque and the 1/6th North Staffords captured the command post in Billiard Copse. Both battalions then stopped and consolidated these positions while the 1/5th Lincolnshires and the 1/4th and 1/5th Leicestershires 'leap-frogged' them and went on to tackle Magny-la-Fosse. These troops were joined by two companies of tanks which had crossed the canal at the Bellicourt tunnel mouth. The fog was now lifting and the tanks and infantry were in full view of the German machine guns and artillery on the higher ground to the east; one

The German command bunkers at la Baraque (no. 38 on map) **were captured by the Staffordshires and used by units of the 46th Division; the photo above shows the Divisional Signal Company with their mascot. The bunker can still be visited (inset). On the day before the above photograph was taken the bunker was used to interrogate German prisoners taken during the Battle of Beaurevoir, and the adjacent bunker was an Advanced Dressing Station for the 91st Field Ambulance. At dusk, with poor light, a German flier flew over and, seeing a group of about 100 soldiers crowded together, dropped six bombs into their midst, not realising they were his countrymen. The majority of the Germans were killed, as were the two Military Police Sergeants with them (both of whom were named Lee) and some of the medics. The British dead from the German bombing are buried in la Baraque Cemetery close by.**

German battery near Etricourt put out of action most of the tanks and held up the advance; the defenders were now more stubborn than before:

> 'Our troops had now reached the enemy's artillery positions, where the German gunners fought gallantly and continued firing their guns up to the last.'[35]

174

Eventually the advance continued and by 3pm the 46th Division had captured Magny-la-Fosse and Lehaucourt, during the day they had taken all of their objectives on time. In addition to the haul of prisoners, over 4,000, and almost a hundred guns, the 46th Division was proud of the fact that they had smashed what was thought to be an impregnable defence line. Their casualties were considered light at about 800, the majority of whom were either wounded or missing. Congratulations flowed in – over the next few days telegrams were sent to the division by the Lord Mayors of towns from which many of the troops came – Walsall, Burton on Trent, Leicester, Stoke on Trent, and the Lord Lieutenant of Leicestershire, followed by various Generals and even Field Marshal Sir Douglas Haig, who did not write directly but passed his appreciation down the line:

'The brilliant achievement of the 46th Division in forcing the passage of the ST QUENTIN CANAL and mastering the defences of a large sector of the famous HINDENBURG Line is worthy of the highest credit.'[36]

The attack to the north of the 46th Division had been carried out by the American 30th Division. This was to be their first major battle and to assist their planning they were attached to the Australian Corps. Their task was to smash the Hindenburg line between Riqueval and Bony and then allow the Australians to pass through and capture Nauroy and the high ground to the north of this village. The Americans started well but had some setbacks and had mixed fortunes. The forward troops entered Bellicourt village and also captured the southern entrance to the canal tunnel, going on to capture Nauroy village. The Americans then found that they had made a major error, which had been made by the British and French Armies many times before. In the exaltation of their success, and with the difficulties in locating all the German dug-out and tunnel entrances, 'mopping-up' of defences had not been carried out. Germans appeared from the canal tunnel (inside the tunnel mouth was a concrete post for four machine guns protecting many barges which barracked hundreds of German troops) and other entrances which had been overlooked and attacked the Americans from the rear, cutting them off. The remnants of the Americans were then joined by the 5th Australian Division, who found that the situation was by now critical as the Germans were putting up stout resistance and counter-attacking. Parties of Americans were found to be isolated and disorganised, to make matters worse the mist then cleared and gave full view to the German artillery and machine gunners; the German defenders – the 121st Division – then strengthened their counter-attacks. An Australian officer, Major Anderson Wark, moved forward alone through the

Blair Anderson Wark VC

artillery and machine gun fire to assess and take control of the situation. Rallying a mixed American and Australian force he led them on to attack and capture a length of the Hindenburg Line trenches and then went on to capture and occupy Nauroy. With a few of his men he rushed a gun battery and captured and killed the crew on the way; for his gallantry and leadership he was awarded the VC.

BELLICOURT AND BELLENGLISE TODAY

Many of the Hindenburg defence posts can still be found, although as in other sectors much is below ground and is therefore effectively hidden. A good example of careful sighting can be found where the N44 crosses the canal; the north abutment is a cleverly sited pill box, sited to cover the canal [**no. 39 on map**].

At la Baraque [**no. 38 on map**] is a small copse in which are several concrete shelters, also in the undergrowth is a deep shaft to some underground shelters. This was a command centre for the German troops, holding this stretch of canal, captured by the 1/5th South Staffs. and made into a report centre. It was the scene of a tragic air raid by a German aeroplane on the evening of 3 October: a group of 70-80 German prisoners were awaiting interrogation when, in the poor light of dusk, the German plane dropped bombs into the middle of the crowd, killing and wounding many. Several British troops, including two Military Police Sergeants named Lee, who were guarding the prisoners, were also killed by the bombs. The British casualties were buried in what became the la Baraque Cemetery which is close by. This cemetery also contains an unusually high proportion of R.A.M.C. personnel.

The bridge at Riqueval, saved from the German attempt to demolish it, still remains; at the eastern end will be found two concrete infantry posts. The banks of the canal here are very pitted and traces of trenches can be discerned in many places. Another example of clever pill box siting can be found further north up the canal, just below the car park at the Napoleon Platform. This was built into the rock batter by the tow path.

The entrance to the canal tunnel was very heavily fortified, the concrete wall which was just inside does not remain but a machine gun aperture can still be seen in the top left corner of the tunnel facing. The concrete pill box, sited to fire to the northwest and guard the approaches along the valley (named Quarry Ravine by the British), is at the top of the cutting and has recently been excavated and cleaned out and can now be entered. Three hundred metres along the embankment from this is a concrete mined machine gun position, [**no. 40 on map**], one which caused the Americans many casualties when they attacked here. This

The bridge where the N44 crosses the canal. The pill box entrance is in the trees on the right, a concrete tunnel leads to the interior of the abutment which is hollow. The machine gun aperture (now blocked in but still evident) was sited to cover the canal.

was in one of the outer trenches of the Hindenburg Line.

Close to Le Tronquoy, a farm which contains several concrete bunkers, the canal disappears into the northern mouth of the le Tronquoy Tunnel. The tunnel housed many Germans who were taken prisoner there. In nearby Fleche Wood, named because of it's arrow-head like shape, is the entrance to a concrete tunnel which ran underground to connect with the front line trenches near the canal. Most of the tunnel length is sealed off, due to roof collapses, the 30-40 metres length still open gives a good idea of the scale of work involved. The wood and the tunnel were cleared by the 15th Highland Light Infantry during the late evening of 29 September 1918.

The American soldier right stands beside a mined machine gun position which caused many casualties to the Americans trying to approach the tunnel mouth. It can still be found today (inset).

A large industrial town on the north bank of the River Somme, St. Quentin was intended by the Germans to be denied to the British on account of its rail junction and the field of view from the buildings in the town centre. The Canal de St. Quentin ran to the east of the town so the *Siegfriedstellung* was sited to the west of the conurbation; the strong defence line here had the advantage of the towns facilities – billetting, rail fed supplies and numerous hidden sitings for artillery and observers. The devastated area to the west gave the British little scope for accommodation or defence.

The Germans fell back through the area in early April 1917, being pursued by the 32nd Division. Their intention was to prevent the British from approaching the Hindenburg Line, and to hold Fayet, Holnon and Francilly-Selency as a forward or outpost line. The 1st Dorsets of the 32nd Division attacked the Germans holding Holnon at dawn on 2 April 1917; they took the village by 6am but were prevented from advancing further by heavy machine gun fire from the edge of a wood around a chateau to the north of Selency. This village and its twin village of Francilly-Selency were the objectives of the 2nd Manchesters, attacking alongside the Dorsets. It was explained to the Manchesters that the villages could be distinguished by the fact that one possessed a spire and the other a tower but as neither village was more than about 8 feet high this information was not of much assistance![37]

The Manchesters swept through Francilly-Selency and evicted the German defenders but as they emerged from the other side they came upon a battery of 77mm field guns firing at them at point blank range. Captain Glover and C Company attacked and captured the battery after hand-to-hand fighting with the German gun crews. Later that night they tried to tow the guns back behind the British lines with dragropes but were unable to do so because of German shelling and the broken ground. Captain Glover was awarded the Military Cross for capturing the guns, as were Second Lieutenants Briggs and Taylor and Regimental Sergeant Major Hastewell. An important gain of the Manchesters during the day was the high ground to the south of Francilly-Selency. Marked on British trench maps as simply '128

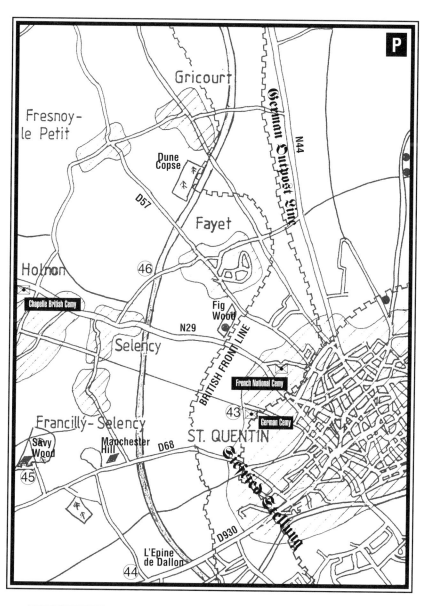

Gricourt

Fresnoy-
le Petit

German Outpost Line

N44

Dune
Copse

D57

Fayet

Holnon

46

Chapelle British Cemy

Fig
Wood

N29

BRITISH FRONT LINE

Selency

French National Cemy

Francilly-Selency

43

German Cemy

Savy
Wood

Manchester
Hill

D68

ST. QUENTIN

45

D930

L'Epine
de Dallon

44

⊔⊓⊔⊓⊔⊓⊔ Main trench line	● Existing structure, British or German, e.g. pill box
◣ Site of interest	
+ Memorial	⊠ Cemeteries

179

metres" it was given on captured German maps as *Margerin Höhe* or Margerine Hill; the Manchesters renamed the position Manchester Hill. Immediately in front of the hill the Germans had constructed a strongpoint in the quarry (Brown Quarry), here the Manchesters captured six German machine guns. Another Manchester battalion, the 16th, was to make Manchester Hill famous almost a year later.

The 2nd Manchesters and 1st Dorsets continued to press and harry the Germans backwards until they were behind the strong defences of the Hindenburg Line. The limit of the advance was a large crater in the road in front of the German wire, blown as a tank stop, beyond this was a salient where the Hindenburg Line jutted out in front of St. Quentin. The British front line was established in the most favourable positions about 200 metres in front of the German trenches but the Germans had sited theirs with the intention of denying the British much choice. The only geographical advantages the British had was the high ground of Manchester Hill, with Brown Quarry behind out of the gaze of German observers.

For the remainder of 1917 this area was quiet, both sides busy on other sectors of the Front and resting divisions took their turn to re-equip and re-organise in comparative safety. The French III Corps held the sector for most of the time, handing over to the British XVIII Corps in mid January 1918. The 61st (South Midlands) Division moved into the area as the French 5th Infantry Division moved out; they were given trench maps, dug-out and billetting details, stores inventories and information on local German movements but considered that while the front line trench was good the support system of trenches and defence works was totally inadequate. Existing strong-points and trenches were kept (including most of the French names) but re-dug and cleaned up; the Royal Engineers of the division, together with artillery, infantry and machine gun units devised a new defence scheme and, when this was approved, the Engineers and infantry working parties began work.

The 61st Division were working on most of the defences in the sector until the 30th Division took over the southern half on 23 February 1918. By now the Germans were expected to attack before long and the infantry battalions of the divisions continued to improve trenches and strongpoints, extending wired areas and organising defence schemes with artillery, trench mortar and machine gun units. The strongpoints or redoubts were sited in accordance with the zonal system of defence; three of the main areas for defence, officially named 'defended localities'. In front of St. Quentin were the hill just north of Francilly-Selency (a maze of trenches named Enghien Redoubt centred around some old buildings named The Cottages and a small quarry) with Fayet village and Fig Wood strongpoints in front of it; the high ground of Manchester Hill with Brown Quarry just behind it and the low rise on the St. Quentin-Ham road, the D930, l'Epine de Dallon. Another main

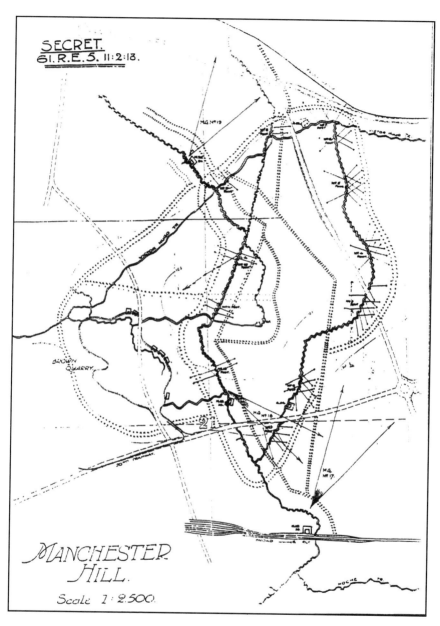

Map of the British defences on Manchester Hill. The site, with its good view of St. Quentin, is today farm land; the quarry was enlarged in later years and is now disused. The hill had been named after the Manchester Regiment who captured it in 1917: the same regiment fought here at the onset of the German 1918 spring offensive.

181

defended locality was Fresnoy-le-Petit. The 61st Division had begun work with infantry working parties of the 2/5th Gloucestershires helping 476 (South Midland) Field Company Royal Engineers bolstering the defences of Manchester Hill, Enghien Redoubt and l'Epine de Dallon. 201 Field Company of the Royal Engineers took over between 23 February and 1 March and continued the wiring on and around Manchester Hill and providing deep dugouts and trench mortar positions around Brown Quarry. For the next three weeks 200 Field Company continued the work, assisted by the 16th Manchesters who were to man the position when attacked. The Manchesters spent much time rehearsing the attack, defence and counter-attack of each position they knew they would have to defend. The Manchesters had been told by their Commanding Officer, Lieutenant-Colonel Wilfrith Elstob, to defend the post to the last man and they knew that when the attack came it would be some time before reinforcements could arrive.

On 19 March the division knew that the German attack would come at any time and so that night they flooded St. Quentin with gas to hinder the Germans massing there. The artillery bombarded known German positions and crossroads over the following day; on the evening of 20 March a thick ground mist began to form in the hollows and around the St. Quentin Canal. A patrol of the Manchesters crept out into No Mans Land during the night of 20/21 March to check if the Germans were concentrating in the front line but found no unusual activity. On Manchester Hill and in the other redoubts the infantry manned their battle positions and made ready. At 4.40am the German barrage began to fall onto the British lines. Gas and high explosive rained down on all positions along the front and rear areas; the men in the redoubt of Manchester Hill and Brown Quarry – the 16th Manchesters with the 2nd Bedfordshires behind them – knew that they would soon be surrounded and would have a desperate struggle on their hands.

Between 9.30am and 3.30pm the Manchesters fought off repeated German attacks, losing men and with ammunition stocks getting low and with telephone communication to divisional headquarters cut off, they launched several counter-attacks, led personally by their Commanding Officer who, firing his revolver and throwing grenades, exhorted his men to fight on. The Germans gradually worked their way to the command post at the crest of the hill, where Lieutenant-Colonel Elstob was killed during the hand-to-hand combat which ensued for the rest of the afternoon. He was posthumously awarded the VC for his actions in defending

Wilfrith Elstob VC the strongpoint and post on the hill, which eventually fell into German hands after they brought field guns up and fired at point blank range into the remaining defenders. The Manchesters in Francilly-Selency had also been fending off repeated attacks but eventually the survivors fell back, leaving many Germans dead.

Other troops of the 30th Division were also in trouble; the 2nd Wiltshires holding l'Epine de Dallon Redoubt – a system of trenches and barbed wire around the ruins of the farm buildings which had stood there – resisted German attacks all morning, being surrounded and with fewer troops able to fight. They were cut off from either reinforcement or a way of retirement: at 1.30pm a carrier pigeon arrived at Divisional H.Q. with a message from Lieutenant-Colonel A.V.P. Martin, saying that he was still holding out in the redoubt with 50 men. One hour later the Germans were in full control of the redoubt and Lieutenant-Colonel Martin and his men were not heard from again.

The 61st Division holding the line in front of Fayet and Gricourt were also under pressure from German attacks. Enghien Redoubt, the strongpoint which had been formed on the rise between Selency and Fayet, incorporating the small quarry there (later to be renamed The Quadrilateral during the fighting at the end of September 1918, when the retreating Germans were to make a stand here) came under fierce pressure. The 2/4th Oxfordshire and Buckinghamshires manning the strongpoint fought off repeated attacks with machine gun and rifle fire, but when field guns were firing at point blank range at them they burnt their papers and retired through the mist and smoke, fighting as they went.

The battle then passed away to the west and for the rest of the summer of 1918 the region was a back area for the Germans.

During September 1918 the Germans were again pushed back to the Hindenburg Line but were putting up a spirited resistance. The 6th Division was on the right flank of the British Fourth Army, where the front joined the French First Army between Holnon and Francilly-Selency. On 18 September the 9th Norfolks and 1st Leicesters were fighting around Holnon but made limited progress because of machine gun fire from German positions on Manchester Hill and The Quadrilateral, two posts which had been British strongpoints in March of that year. Germans in Selency also held up the advance and the 6th Division could not make much progress on that day. It was evening on 19 September before Holnon was in British hands although the Germans in The Quadrilateral could not be dislodged and the French were also unable to capture Manchester Hill. The line was static for several days while the 6th Division made ready for another go and the Germans bolstered their defences. The British were determined to occupy the two areas of high ground because of the view it gave them of the main defences of the Hindenburg Line, which was the next objective. At 5am on 24 September the 6th Division again attacked The Quadrilateral and Selency, this time with a fresh battalion of tanks. The Germans expected the attack and were ready; it was several hours before the British gained a footing on the high ground and they had to fight for it yard by yard. At nightfall the crest was still in German hands until a moonlight attack by the 1st Leicesters secured the position although it would be another two days before the trench system on the hill was fully cleared of Germans. The 1st Division, to the north of the 6th, took Fresnoy-le-Petit and then Gricourt after suffering heavy losses during repeated German counter-attacks.

During the day the French captured Francilly-Selency but were still unable to take possession of Manchester Hill. This they eventually managed to do on the morning of 26 September.

The attackers then had full observation over the Hindenburg Line and plans were made for the major assault. The junction of the British Fourth and French First Armies was adjusted to just south of Fayet. The 6th Division was to attack from in front of Gricourt but the troops, exhausted and weakened by a fortnight of almost continual fighting, were unable to advance and were that night relieved by the French, who went on to press the Germans back to the outpost line, from where they had emerged on 21 March to launch their Spring Offensive. It was to be another three days of fighting before the French were to break through the Hindenburg Line and occupy St. Quentin.

THE AREA TODAY

Few signs or traces of the German or British defences or the hard fighting in the area can be found today; most of the Hindenburg Line has been swallowed up in the later construction of domestic and commercial buildings in and around St. Quentin. Many cellars and underground chambers were strengthened by German engineers but these are today private premises. A large concrete bunker from the front line, the sole survivor of many here, is on the edge of the shopping centre on the northern edge of town. Further out, by the D8 at Omissy, can be found a large artillery observation post with underground chamber, reduced in height by shell fire the remains show the thickness and strength of the walls [**no. 42 on map**]. Close by is a concrete shelter, probably a munitions store for a gun battery.

The French military cemetery on the Selency road from St. Quentin, the N29, stands on the site of the Hindenburg Line.

The German military cemetery, down the old roman road out of town, and difficult to find although signposted, stood in No Mans Land between the German and British front lines. It was begun by the Germans shortly after they took St. Quentin on 28 August 1914, and used by them for the next four years. Their retirement to the Hindenberg Line left the cemetery 200 metres in front of the line, in a depression called Camel Valley, overlooked by both sides. The original grave markers and stone memorial have been replaced but the two large brass warriors on the memorial are original, being cast and placed there in 1915. [**no. 43 on map**].

The British front line and posts have all disappeared, being mainly on agricultural land. The strongpoint of l'Epine de Dallon, where the 2nd Wiltshires fought and disappeared, is today a small cluster of farm buildings and houses [**no. 44 on map**]; its location shows the origin of the name, the road is the spine of the high ground above Dallon village. Manchester Hill, captured by the Manchesters in 1917 and lost by them in 1918, shows no evidence of defences or the struggle there although the siting of the strongpoint can be appreciated. With commanding views over the ground in front of St. Quentin and the city buildings full observation of movement in the streets can be made, even the details of the cathedral can be easily seen. Brown Quarry was worked and enlarged after the war, and was later partly filled in. Rubble found around the crest of the hill is likely to be from these later operations, and no traces of the many dugouts in the quarry exist.

Access to the redoubt was via a long communication trench named Victor Hugo Alley, which ran through Savy Wood to the quarry and the front line. Use of the communication trench was necessary because the land was in full view of observers in St. Quentin although the trees of the wood gave some cover. The extent of the wood is today reduced but Victor Hugo Alley, down which the survivors of the fighting at Manchester Hill escaped, is still evident. [**no. 45 on map**].

The site of Enghien Redoubt [**no. 46 on map**] also shows no sign of its former importance, the ruins on top of the hill, where The Cottages stood, are from recent times and the small quarry is now the site of a domestic dwelling. The site of the German machine guns which held up British attacks in April, 1917 and September, 1918 on the southern edge of the wood, by the N29, shows the advantages of the position and the ground which was swept by the German machine gunners.

Fig Wood, in front of which ran the British front line, was a forward post manned by the 2nd Worcestershires. It was strongly wired with trenches, machine guns and an observation post with telephone link to gun batteries in the rear. It was one of the first posts to be attacked and fall on the morning of 21 March 1918. It is also today one of the few locations of the British forward defences to be found. The actual front line, which was 250 metres to the east, is occupied today by the Mammouth Supermarket and adjacent commercial buildings. Access to the wood is via a track from Fayet; in the wood the trenches of Isigny Alley and Ivry Alley are still evident, though shallow, also to be found is the steel roof of a collapsed elephant iron dugout, the location of one of the machine guns defending the wood. The broken ground in the wood shows that it was heavily shelled, obviously an important target for the German artillery.

Q
VILLERS OUTRÉAUX AND LESDAIN

The Hindenburg Support, also named the Le Catelet-Nauroy Line, was taken by battalions of the 38th (Welsh) Division. Having been held up and unable to advance because of the German defenders, they found the line evacuated on the morning of 5 October 1918. They moved through and beyond the defences but could not proceed further because the Germans had organised themselves behind the Masniéres-Beaurevoir Line (*Siegfried II Stellung*), which ran through Mortho Wood. The line had been sited here because of the open countryside giving a clear field of fire to machine guns in the small woods and copses. Many concrete pill boxes had been built before the 1918 spring offensive and the barbed wire was in thick entanglements, several lines deep.

Three days later the Welshmen were to try and force the Beaurevoir Line and enter Villers Outréaux; a night attack was considered the best bet and began at 1am. The defences of the line proved to be a major obstacle, Mortho Wood could not be approached because of machine gun fire although a toe-hold was gained south of the wood, opposite Villers Outréaux. At 5am the 2nd Welch Fusiliers passed through this gap and, as three tanks arrived to help (one of which fired on the Welch), worked their way into Villers Outréaux. The capture of this village is described in *The War the Infantry Knew*.[38]

The Welch Regiment and the Welsh Fusiliers had another go at the Germans in the Beaurevoir Line around Mortho Wood and after hard fighting in the trenches they overcame the resistance and won their objectives.

Meanwhile the line north of Mortho Wood was being attacked by the 21st Division. Resistance was very patchy, machine gun crews in some pill boxes held out until overpowered whilst others retired as British troops approached and after several hours the line was in British hands. The 2nd Lincolnshires moved their battalion headquarters up to the line, in a pill box just behind where Angles Cemetery now is. The 2nd Lincs then continued the attack; at first they were unable to advance to Angle Wood and were held up there but Angles Chateau, which sits atop a ridge, fell, and was then retaken by the Germans, who in turn were forced out again.

The 1st Lincolnshires had also been pressing the Germans back with

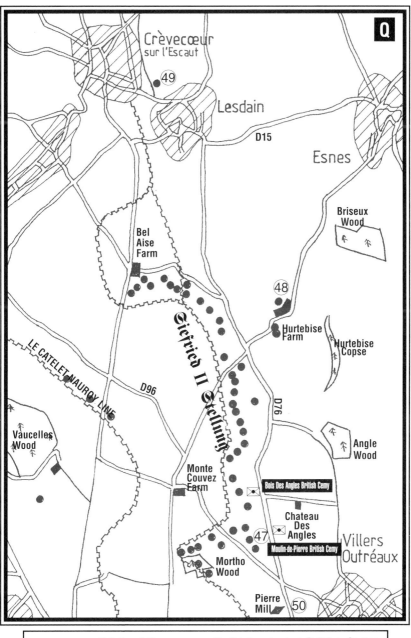

Crèvecœur
sur l'Escaut

49

Lesdain

D15

Esnes

Briseux
Wood

Bel
Aise
Farm

48

Hurtebise
Farm

Hurtebise
Copse

LE CATELET-NAUROY LINE

Siegfried II Stellung

D96

Vaucelles
Wood

D76

Angle
Wood

Monte
Couvez
Farm

Bois Des Angles British Cemy

Chateau
Des
Angles

47

Villers
Outréaux

Moulin-de-Pierre British Cemy

Mortho
Wood

Pierre
Mill   50

ᴗᴖᴗᴖᴗᴖ Main trench line

◣ Site of interest

✝ Memorial

● Existing structure, British or German,
e.g. pill box

⊠ Cemeteries

This German strongpoint bunker besides the D96, with thick steel observation plate, was used by the Germans who stopped the Welsh advance and prevented them from taking the Beaurevoir Line around Mortho Wood. It held out for three days until the Welsh attacked again, during the night of 8 October 1918. (marked 47 on map).

mixed success. At 8am they were held up by a party of Germans who had dug in at a strongpoint at Hurtebise Wood. The Germans were pounded with one of their own field guns which had been captured, together with two British field guns and a light trench mortar. The garrison held out for some time but eventually surrendered. Another strongpoint was at Hurtebise Farm, the Germans here were also putting up a determined resistance. Machine guns in a pill box prevented the British from taking the farm until infantrymen of the 1st Essex, with the help of a tank and four Lewis guns, rushed the pill box and captured the machine gun crews.

The area was then consolidated; the 1st Hertfords advanced to take Briseux Wood, but once it was reached they had difficulty passing through the trees and bushes, slowly forcing a way through to the eastern edge.

The trenches and pill boxes of the Beaurevoir Line formed a salient around Bel Aise Farm, this was the objective of the 10th Royal Fusiliers ('The Stockbrokers') who also were attacking at 1am. The Fusiliers found that the two strong wire systems had not been sufficiently cut by the artillery barrage and they had great difficulty in getting through in the dark. They came under fire from machine guns in concrete posts in the line which should also have been destroyed in the barrage; these had to be overcome and the German gunners were killed or taken prisoner. A few pill boxes were missed in the darkness and confusion of the battle, which were mopped-up by the 1st Essex who took 30 Germans prisoner.

188

Hurtebise Farm is sited on a slight ridge and the Germans formed a strongpoint here, with a pill box with five loopholes, covering each direction. After the Germans had made a stand at this spot the 1st Essex captured the pill box.

Lesdain was garrisoned by the German Jäger Division and the New Zealand Division was given the task of clearing them out. On the north of Lesdain the defenders put up a strong resistance before being overpowered. The New Zealanders then worked forward to take Esnes, where they fought off a counter-attack without too much difficulty.

THE AREA TODAY

Most of the dense cluster of pill boxes which formed the main defences of the Beaurevoir Line still exist although, being built at trench level, often the only indication of their existence is a small concrete roof or a patch of coarse grass and weeds. Several of those captured by the Welshmen can be found around Mortho Wood and Angles Cemetery. Those which formed the Bel Aise salient and were fought over by the Royal Fusiliers can also be found but are on private land. The strongpoint of Hurtebise Farm pill box is also still standing [**no. 48 on map**] but also is on private property.

The village of Esnes, with its castle, is different to those to the west: the land and villages to the east of here did not form any of the fixed defence schemes and saw only mobile warfare in 1914 and late October and November 1918. The houses and buildings were largely undamaged and many are of great age, which gives a different character to those to the west which were mainly rebuilt in the 1920's and 30's.

In Lesdain Mill the Germans had sited a machine gun post with a strong concrete bunker for the crew. The position caused a problem to the New Zealanders of the 1st Battalion who had passed it in the dark until Sergeant R.J. Sinclair rushed and killed the crew and secured the ruins and post. Three hundred Germans were taken prisoner in the village. The mill ruins were cleared but the bunker still remains. (no. 49 on map)

Pierre Mill, by the side of the D76 near Villers Outréaux, marked no. 50 on map, occupied a dominant position and was made a strongpoint by the Germans. Surrounded by wire and trenches, several machine guns sited here held up the advance of the 38th (Welsh) Division on 8 October, 1918. The 2nd Royal Welch Fusiliers were fired on from here and returned the fire with Lewis guns. After a while the German garrison fled the mill and ran off.

R
JONCOURT AND BEAUREVOIR

After the 46th (North Midland) Division had crossed the Canal du Nord between Bellicourt and Bellenglise on 29 September 1918 the 32nd Division passed through them and continued to press the attack. To the north the Australian Corps and the Americans had been having some difficulty around the tunnel entrance and Gouy had not been reached.

Plans were made to capture Joncourt on 1 October, at 8am the 15th Lancashire Fusiliers (1st Salford Pals) attacked the village from the south while the 32nd Australian Battalion tried to enter from the west. Most of the Germans had retired from the village to the Beaurevoir Line on the high ground to the east but had left behind a determined rear guard of the 80th Infantry Regiment who were to hold on tenaciously. The Salfords came under artillery and machine gun fire from pill boxes in the village, they cleared the houses during the morning but could not pass its eastern edge. The defenders who were not killed escaped to their own lines, only eight falling prisoner to the British.

The pill box on the southern outskirts of Joncourt, taken by the Salford Pals on 1 October 1918. On one wall is the remains of a small cement plaque in Germanic script but this is no longer legible.

During the late afternoon another attack was launched, on the main trenches of the Beaurevoir Line after an artillery barrage consisting of high explosive, shrapnel and smoke shells which lasted through the day. The southern end of the line was attacked by the 5/6th Royal Scots and the 1/5th Borderers, accompanied by 16 Mark V tanks. Both battalions fought through the German defences and took their objectives but were driven back by German counter-attacks. The 1/5th Borderers had taken the small cluster of buildings at Preselles but were unable to hold on to them because of intense machine gun fire.

The 2nd Manchesters had advanced to take the Beaurevoir Line on the high ground east of Joncourt. At 4pm they began working up the rising ground to the trenches on the hill top, which in parts were incomplete and dug to only 300mm deep but contained numerous rifle and machine gun pits. Forward movement was difficult because of very thick wire. Four tanks were used to make passages through the wire with another five to help clear the trenches and machine guns. Stiff hand-to-hand fighting ensued over the next three hours. The line of pill boxes on the crest were taken from the Germans one by one and at 7pm the ruins of Swiss Cottage (now known as Moulin Grison Farm) were in Mancunian hands. Losses were incurred: five killed, 85 wounded and seven missing, with 150 German prisoners. This foothold in the Beaurevoir Line was of great value to the British and of this the Germans were fully aware. They made repeated counter-attacks during the night but the Manchesters held on to the position with the help of the 15th Lancashire Fusiliers who had come up from Joncourt.

The Beaurevoir Line at Préselles was still in German hands and another attempt to take it from them was launched at 6.05am on 3 October. The South and North Staffordshires of the 46th Division suffered many casualties from machine guns in the concrete emplacements on either side of the Ramicourt Road during the approach. C and D Companies of the 1/6th South Staffordshires were the first to reach the German trenches, followed by A and B Companies. Several officers were killed in the close fighting around the pill boxes and progress faltered until the 1/5th South Staffordshires reinforced them. C Company under Captain Meynell took many of the posts on the northern side of the road; the Battalion War Diary[39] records an unusually high usage of bayonets during the fighting. The troops then pressed on towards Ramicourt, the Germans attempted to hold the village but were forced out by infantry and tanks. The 1/5th Sherwood Foresters captured the pill boxes (**marked 51 on map**) on the northern flank of the Staffordshires, adjacent to those captured two days earlier by the 2nd Manchesters; during the fighting for these emplacements Sergeant Johnson captured two machine gun positions which held up his platoon, bayonetting the gunners, and was awarded the VC.

The 32nd Division had meanwhile cleared Sequehart to the south,

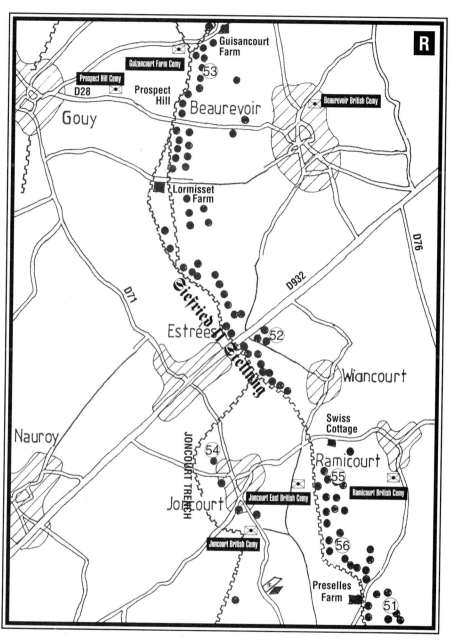

R

Guisancourt Farm

Guizancourt Farm Cemy

Prospect Hill Cemy

D28

Prospect Hill

Gouy

Beaurevoir

Beaurevoir British Cemy

53

Lormisset Farm

D76

Siegfried Stellung

D932

Estrées

52

Wiancourt

Nauroy

Swiss Cottage

JONCOURT TRENCH

54

Ramicourt

55

Ramicourt British Cemy

D71

Joncourt East British Cemy

Joncourt

56

Joncourt British Cemy

Preselles Farm

51

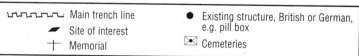

	Main trench line		Existing structure, British or German, e.g. pill box
	Site of interest		
	Memorial		Cemeteries

193

the 1st Dorsets entering the village at 7.45am, but the Germans launched a major counter-attack immediately. To hold the ground won A Company under Lieutenant Lonsdale bayonet charged the Germans, killing many and driving the rest back. The Germans attacked again; the Dorsets fell back to the edge of the village then went forward again and re-took the village, capturing 360 prisoners and 25 machine guns.

Estrées had been a strongly fortified village in front of the main defence line. The 56th Australian Battalion followed tanks into the village on 1 October, Lieutenant Watt and his troops drove out the remaining rear guard of the 119th Division. The main defence line to the east of Estrées was attacked by the 18th and 19th Australian Battalions; as they passed through they were fired on from the rear by Germans of the 81st Infantry Regiment in the last houses. As they reached the wire of the Beaurevoir Line they came under heavy machine and field gun fire from the concrete pill boxes. Those on the north of the road (the D932) were taken by the 19th Battalion but the 18th Battalion, on the southern side of the road, found the wire to be much thicker than normal, with six belts each of 7-8 metres width, and insurmountable. A few Australians managed to pass through the wire; Lieutenant Maxwell of the 18th pushed through single handed and captured two machine guns, killing the crews. He was taken prisoner but escaped after shooting his guards with a concealed pistol. He was awarded the VC for his exploits. The Germans in the positions behind the wire took a heavy toll on the Australians who tried to work down the defences from the road and the attack was halted for a half hour while the emplacements were subjected to an artillery bombardment. The group of pill boxes (**no. 52 on map**) were then attacked from the north by the 19th Battalion, who took 200 prisoners and 18 machine guns.

The emplacements around Lormisset Farm were rushed by the 26th Battalion, who worked up the trench from pill box to pill box, most held 10-12 men of the 119th Division, many of these fled.

Gouy and Le Catelet, which had so far been denied to the British, and Prospect Hill, between Gouy and Beaurevoir, were to be taken by troops of the 50th (Northumbrian) Division. The two villages were to be cleared by the 4th King's Royal Rifle Corps. The task was not easy: after five hours of stubborn fighting the German 54th Division was driven out of the villages except for small parties which held out in the cellars and dug-outs. The Battalion War Diary records that:

> 'the enemy fought with a determination to which their dead left in the captured positions bear witness. Both villages had been fortified with great skill and thoroughness.'[40]

The Germans were not happy with the loss of Gouy and at 1pm the 21st Reserve Division pressed back into the village, forcing the British back; the 2nd Northumberland Fusiliers entered the fray and drove the

One of the pill boxes, with steel observation post, at Lormisset Farm, shortly after it was taken by the Australians, above, and today, right. The underground chamber held 12 men.

Germans from the village which then remained in British hands.

The high ground of Prospect Hill was the objective of the 6th Royal Inniskilling Fusiliers; working up the slope they came under fire from within Gouy and veered off to deal with this, so the 1st King's Own Yorkshire Light Infantry took over and won the crest of the Hill. The Australians of the 26th Battalion had meanwhile been working up the Beaurevoir Line, the pill boxes between Lormisset Farm and the Gouy-Beaurevoir road (the D28) fell easily but the Australians then met determined opposition and their progress stopped just short of the eastern crest. Machine guns in and around the concrete emplacements and field guns at Guisancourt Farm were the stumbling blocks, and on the following day (October 4) the 9th Devonshires of the 25th Division tried to clear them, a few pill boxes (**marked 53 on map**) were taken and they approached Beaucourt, but the gains were small and at the end of the day Guisancourt was not reached. The 25th Division resumed the attack again on the following morning, 5 October. The 20th Manchesters managed to get into Beaurevoir but suffered so many casualties in doing so that they could not remain and fell back at mid-day until the 1/5th Gloucestershires resumed the attack at 6.30pm; they swept into the village and took the resting German garrison by surprise and dug in to the east.

Still inhabited, this bunker at Joncourt was one of the many posts for artillery observation, giving good views over the British lines (no. 54 on map).

Still the defenders of Guisancourt Farm held out, until a surprise attack by the 11th Sherwood Foresters at 4am on 6 October, 195 prisoners being taken there. After three days of continuous fighting the Battle of the Beaurevoir Line was over.

THE AREA TODAY

In the village of Joncourt are two pill boxes which were taken by the Australians on 1 October 1918, together with an observation post which is still inhabited during the warmer months (no. 54 on map). On the southern side of the village, by the Levergies road, the D71, is a concrete pill box which, manned by rear guard machine gun crews, held up the Salford Pals before being overwhelmed.

Evidence of American occupation can also be found. The Mairie, in the village centre, was used by the 27th and 30th American Divisions as headquarters during the battle for Brancourt on 8 October and later; by the entrance can be found the following inscription:

Rear Echelon

AMER. DIV.

Headquarters

Most of the pill boxes of the Beaurevoir Line which held up the British still survive and can be found, although most were constructed at trench level and only the roofs are evident. They can be difficult to locate when crops are more than 200- 300mm high. The first ones to be captured, by the 2nd Manchesters, are directly up the slope facing Joncourt East Cemetery (which holds many of those who fell taking them), **marked 55**

on map. Just south of these are those captured by the 1/5th Sherwood Foresters, where Sergeant Johnson won his VC (**no. 56 on map**). The fields around Préselles Farm still hold those on either side of the road taken by the 1/5th South Staffordshires.

East of Estrées is the line of emplacements taken by the 18th and 19th Australians, the group on the south side of the road are those which held out and where Lieutenant Maxwell VC was taken prisoner and escaped. Lormisset Farm still has a number of concrete emplacements, some of which have steel observation slits. From here the line of pill boxes continues to Prospect Hill, those which stalled the Australians and the 9th Devonshires lead to Guisancourt Farm, the last section of the Beaurevoir Line to fall.

William Henry Johnson VC

Joseph Maxwell VC

The pill boxes which held up the Australian advance at Estrées, and where Lieutenant Maxwell won his VC after escaping from the Germans, can still be found when not hidden by crops. (*Below*)

Most of the emplacements for the Beaurevoir Line were at trench level and can therefore be difficult to locate. The one left was one of those taken by D Company of the 2nd Manchesters, one of whose officers was the poet Wilfrid Owen. The Manchesters consolidated their position around the pill boxes, from where Owen fired a captured machine gun at the Germans, an act for which he was awarded the MC.

S

THE REAR AREAS

To the east of Cambrai and St Quentin were the main German supply and store areas, where materials were off-loaded from rail and canal transport, and goods to be sent back to Germany, such as guns and arms for repair and requisitioned scrap metals were loaded. Some train depots were entraining and detraining stations for troop movements.

Between Iwuy and Thun-St Martin, northeast of Cambrai, was a very busy transport area where a network of light gauge rail lines converged. Some industrial warehouses were used for storage; unloading points for the normal gauge railway and Escaut Canal took up much of the land and were a target for British air bombing raids. As a precaution the Germans built concrete shelters for troops and military transport workers, together with some machine gun pill boxes for defence. Most of these shelters were demolished when factories were built here in later years but some were left standing and can be visited.

In the hilly and wooded area around St Quentin were many

This house by the side of the main road, the N30, conceals a strong, bomb proof shelter constructed by the Germans. Inhabited until recent years, the house was good camouflage from aerial observation. Entry to the shelter is through the back door, over which is an inscription in the concrete:
ERBAUT VON DER K.G.L. WÜRTTENB. EISE. BET. KOMP. 98, MAI 1917

observation posts looking out over the British lines, up to ten kilometres away. From these vantage points observers, aided by powerful telescopes, could watch troop movements and guide artillery even in

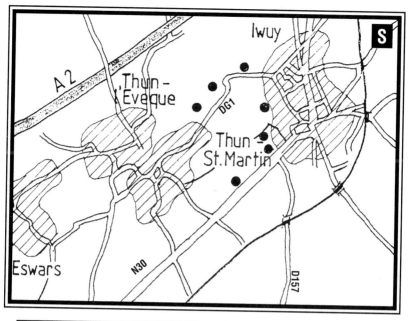

Key:
- ⊔⊓⊔⊓⊔⊓ Main trench line
- ◢ Site of interest
- ✝ Memorial
- ● Existing structure, British or German, e.g. pill box
- ⊠ Cemeteries

poor light conditions. The British were aware of most of these posts and targetted them with counter fire but had limited success.

Some of these observation posts have survived and the visitor can appreciate the advantage held by the German artillery. North of Homblières, on the edge of Diana's Wood, and hidden from British eyes by Diana's Hill, is a tall concrete observation tower giving clear views to the west.

Good observation was obtained from the high hill crowned by Maple Copse, to the southeast of Homblières. The Germans made use of the natural feature and watched the British across St Quentin from trenches on top of the hill. The hill top – the highest around – still contains

The tall observation tower on the edge of Diana's Wood. From the top chamber an artillery observer could see over the hill to the front lines and the British rear areas. This tower, together with the one at Homblières, would have been used to watch the destruction of the British 30th Division on Manchester Hill on the morning of 21 March 1918

This observation post by the N29 in Homblières was built into a mill which stood here. The brickwork gave good camouflage. The post gives good views over the British lines on the other side of St Quentin although tall modern buildings now obscure the view.

the now shallow trenches and shell holes, also here is a mined dugout which has recently collapsed.

By the D57 near Neuville St Amand is another observation post, due to its location height was not needed but protection for the artillery observer was. At nearby Itancourt is another of the artillery observation posts in the area.

At Croix-Fonsommes the Germans had a large rail siding where ammunition and supplies were transferred from main line to narrow gauge rail wagons. A strong concrete shelter was started but halted when the British attacked at Cambrai in 1917. The bunker was not finished, and its part built condition today gives a good idea of the construction method.

One of the last German defence lines passed le Cateau, where a stand was made at the end of October 1918. Just north of le Cateau is the village of Montay, which was on the junction of the British Third and Fourth Armies. A natural defence line here, the River Selle with a high railway embankment on the east side, was exploited by the German defenders, who had built some pill boxes. Welshmen of the 38th Division forced their way across the river during the night of 20 October, coming under heavy fire from machine guns in the pill boxes and other machine guns on the rail embankment. Two of the pill boxes which had to be captured can still be found by the river and railway.

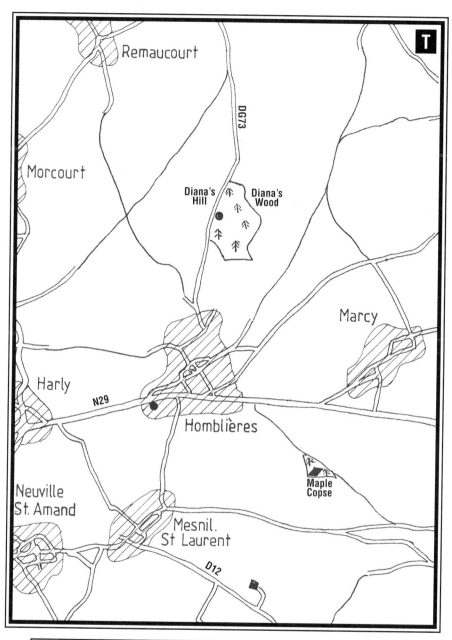

T

Remaucourt

DG73

Morcourt

Diana's
Hill

Diana's
Wood

Marcy

Harly

N29

Homblières

Maple
Copse

Neuville
St. Amand

Mesnil.
St Laurent

D12

 Main trench line
 Site of interest
 Memorial

● Existing structure, British or German,
  e.g. pill box
 Cemeteries

At Croix-Fonsommes the Germans had a large rail siding where ammunition and supplies were transferred from main line to narrow gauge rail wagons. A strong concrete shelter was started but halted when the British attacked at Cambrai in 1917. The bunker was not finished, and its part built condition today gives a good idea of the construction method.

Between the river and the railway near Montay, this is one of the surviving two pill boxes taken by the Welshmen.

One of the many sheltered observation posts which the Germans built to maintain artillery supremacy (see map, pages 44, 45). All were sited to give excellent views over the British front, rear and transport lines. From within the observers directed their artillery and watched British movements. This one is to the south of St Quentin.

Pen & Sword Books Limited

FREEPOST SF5

47 Church Street

BARNSLEY

South Yorkshire

S70 2BR

Leo Cooper

Would you like to receive information about other Pen & Sword Books?

Please fill in your name and address below:

Mr/Mrs/Ms ....

Address ....

....

.... Postcode ....

Please use block capitals

Trade enquiries please tick [ ]   Telephone: 01226 734555

Please tick your areas of interest:

Pre World War One	[ ]	World War Two	[ ]	Regimental History	[ ]
Napoleonic	[ ]	Post World War Two	[ ]	Military Reference	[ ]
World War One	[ ]	Falklands	[ ]	Military Biography	[ ]

Leo Cooper

FURTHER READING

Many divisions and regiments saw action in the area which is covered by this book; the many battles and actions in front of and behind the Hindenburg Line appear in the history of many of those involved. Some of the information is scant and sketchy, although some histories are rich in detail with maps, dates, movements and results. Some also include stories of humour and tragedy; most give glowing reports of acts of bravery, heroism and tenacity by the troops involved. Most of the divisional and regimental histories were written in the years immediately following the Great War and are now difficult to obtain. A wealth of personal memoirs exists, written by both the great and good, and those on the ground or in the trenches. As with the divisional and regimental histories, recollections of times spent in the area can be interesting and informative.

The Official Histories of the war (most volumes have now been republished or are available through public libraries) give information on actions and the units involved. The battles in the region have also continued to produce a number of books in later years: Some books have covered the events on a large scale, illustrating strategy, others have concerned themselves more with events in smaller areas or more detailed actions. The books below will all provide further information on events in the area.

1918, The Last Act. B. Pitt, pub. Cassell, London 1962.
The Ironclads of Cambrai. B. Cooper, pub, Souvenir, London 1967.
See How They Ran, The British Retreat of 1918. pub. Leo Cooper, London 1970.
The Kaisers Battle, 21 March 1918: The First Day of the Spring Offensive.
    M. Middlebrook, pub. Allen Lane London 1978.
Cheerful Sacrifice, The Battle of Arras 1917. pub. Leo Cooper, London 1993.

REFERENCES

1. *A Wood Called Bourlon, The Cover-up after Cambrai, 1917.* William Moore,
    pub. Leo Cooper, London 1988.
2. *Cambrai, The First Great Tank Battle 1917.* A.J. Smithers,
    pub. Leo Cooper, London 1992.
3. *The Fifth Army.* General Sir Hubert Gough,
    pub. Hodder and Stoughton, London 1931.
4. *Official History of Australia in the War of 1914-18.* vol. IV,1917.
    C.E.W. Bean, pub. Angus and Robertson, Sydney 1943.
5. *Storm of Steel.* Ernst Jünger.
    pub. Chatto and Windus, London 1929.
6. *Hints on Reconnaissance for Mines and Land Mines in the Area
    Evacuated by the Germans.* Army Printing and Stationery
    Services, May 1917.
7. Report of Commander Royal Engineers, 11th Division, First Army.
8. Report of 182 Tunnelling Company, Royal Engineers.
9. *Official History of the War, France and Belgium, 1917* vol 1.
    C. Falls 1940.

10. Syllabus for Royal Engineers Training School, Rouen. Work of
  R.E. in war of 1914-19, Miscellaneous. pub. Instition of Royal
  Engineers, Chatham 1927.
11. *Official History of the War, France and Belgium, 1917*, vol 1 ibid.
12. *Canadian Expeditionary Force 1914-19.* G.W.L. Nicholson,
  Ottowa 1962.
13. Queen Victoria's Rifles 1792-1922. C.A.C. Keeson.
  pub. Constable, London 1923.
14. Jünger, ibid.
15. *History of the 123rd (Grenadier) Regiment, Württemburg.*
  (quoted in Bean, 1917.)
16. Bean, 1917. ibid.
17. *Memoirs of an Infantry Officer.* Siegfried Sassoon,
  pub. Faber, London 1930.
18. War Diary, 18th Battalion, Manchester Regiment.
19. Jünger, ibid.
20. *The 42nd (East Lancashire) Division 1914-1918.* F.P. Gibbon,
  pub. Country Life, London 1920.
21. *A History of the East Lancashire Royal Engineers.* Members of the Corps,
  pub. Country Life, London 1921.
22. War Diary, 2/7th Battalion, West Yorkshire Regiment.
23. *The 8th Division in War, 1914-1918.* Boraston and Bax,
  pub. Medici Society, London 1926.
24. War Diary, 7th Battalion Leicestershire Regiment.
25. *The Cambridgeshires 1914 to 1919.* E. Riddel and M. Clayton,
  pub. Bowes and Bowes, London 1934.
26. War Diary, 6th Battalion, Royal West Kent Regiment.
27. *History of the 12th (Eastern) Division in the Great War.*
  Major-General Sir Arthur Scott and P. Middleton Brumwell,
  pub. Nesbit, London 1923.
28. 42nd Division, ibid.
29. *History of the 107th Infantry U.S.A..* G.F. Jacobson, pub.
  Seventh Regiment Armory, New York 1920.
30. 107th Infantry, ibid.
31. Jünger, ibid.
32. East Lancashire Engineers, ibid.
33. Report appended to War Diary, 1/5th Battalion, South
  Staffordshire Regiment.
34. South Staffs, ibid.
35. *Breaking the Hindenburg Line. History of the 46th (North
  Midlands) Division.* R.E. Priestley, pub. Unwin, London 1919.
36. South Staffs, ibid.
37. Report appended to War Diary, 2nd Battalion, Manchester Regiment.
38. *The War the Infantry Knew.* J.C. Dunn, pub. Janes, London 1987.
39. 1/5th South Staffs, ibid.
40. War Diary, 4th Battalion Kings Royal Rifle Corps

INDEX

Peters, Lieutenant 9
Pierre Mill 190
Préselles 192
Pronville 89
Prospect Farm 86,88
Prospect Hill 194

Quarry Wood 106
Quéant 89,92,93
Quennemont Farm 160
Quennet Copse 164
Quesnoy 98

Rambo, Second Lieutenant Ben M. 162
Reed, Lance-Corporal, DCM 128
Rethel 19
Ribécourt-la-Tour 126,133
Riqueval 171,173
Robertson, General 17
Ronssoy 136
Rouex 59,64
Rupprecht, Crown Prince 22
Ryan, Private 69
Rye's plates 139,144,145

Sailly-en-Ostravent 79,84
St. Quentin 9,178,202
Sauchicourt 98
Sauchy Cauchy 97
Sauchy Lestrée 97,98
Sexton, Sergeant M.V. VC 170
Shepherd, Rifleman A.E. VC 129
Shirley, Second Lieutenant S.M. 74
Siegfriedstellung 19,22,28
Smart, Second Lieutenant J.E. 74
Smith, Lieutenant 56
Stone, Captain W.N. VC 102,103
Swiss Cottage 192

Tadpole Copse 100,106
Taillander, Albert 24
La Terrière 163,164
Thun-St.-Martin 198
Tilloy-les-Mofflaines 50,53
Totham Paton, Captain G.H. VC 130

Trescault 20,113
Le Tronquoy 177
Trenches:
    Balcony 89
    Bovis 71
    Canal 105
    Donner Weg 103
    Edda Weg 103
    Farmers Lane 78
    Isigny 185
    Ivry 13,185
    Kaiser 133
    Knuckle 71,75
    Muck 17
    Piccadilly 65
    Rats Tail 102
    Tower 71
    Triangle 17,56
    Tunnel 72,75
    Ulster 78
    Unseen 108,133,134
    Victor Hugo 185

La Vaquerie 128
Vann, Lietenant-Colonel B.W. VC 171
Vaucelles 157,158,159
Vaucellete Farm 138,141,144
Vendhuile 160,163
Le Verguier 169,170
Villeret 169
Villers Guislain 136,138
Villers Outréaux 186,190
Villers Plouich 128,132
Vis-en-Artois 79, 83
Vitry-en-Artois

Wagner, Wilhelm Richard 20,22
Waller, Private H. VC 74
Wancourt 59,60
Wark, Major B. Anderson VC 175
Welsh Ridge 146,157
Westphal, Second Lieutenant B.A. 74
Woods, Private J.P. VC 170
Wotanstellung 20,22,39,79,89,90

Zwischenstellung 27,31,40,47